HISTORIC MONTEREY

Anita Yasuda

Schiffer Publishing Ltd®

4880 Lower Valley Road, Atglen, Pennsylvania 19310

Dedication

This work is dedicated to my daughter,
who shares my passion for history.

Other Schiffer Books by Anita Yasuda:
Traditional Kimono Silks
Japanese Anime Linens: 1970s to Present
Japanese Children's Fabrics: 1950s-1970s

Copyright © 2008 by Anita Yasuda
Library of Congress Control Number: 2007939518

Designed by Martha Tyzenhouse
Type set in New Baskerville BT / Humanist521 BT
ISBN: 978-0-7643-2871-8
Printed in China

Schiffer Books are available at special discounts for bulk purchases for sales promotions or premiums. Special editions, including personalized covers, corporate imprints, and excerpts can be created in large quantities for special needs. For more information contact the publisher:

Published by Schiffer Publishing Ltd.
4880 Lower Valley Road
Atglen, PA 19310
Phone: (610) 593-1777; Fax: (610) 593-2002
E-mail: Info@schifferbooks.com

For the largest selection of fine reference books on this and related subjects, please visit our web site at
www.schifferbooks.com
We are always looking for people to write books on new and related subjects. If you have an idea for a book please contact us at the above address.

This book may be purchased from the publisher.
Include $3.95 for shipping.
Please try your bookstore first.
You may write for a free catalog.

In Europe, Schiffer books are distributed by
Bushwood Books

Contents

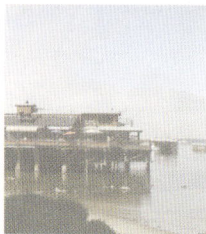

Acknowledgments

This book was an independent project into the historic buildings and places in Monterey, but it would not be have been possible without the help of the California Department of Parks and Recreation, Monterey History & Art Association, and the dedication of countless volunteers who work tirelessly to preserve Monterey's historic places.

In addition:
Colton Hall Museum
Monterey City Library
Bancroft Library, Berkeley
The United States Library of Congress

Fishing Fleet, Monterey. Pub. Bell Magazine Agency.

Preface

The Bay of Monterey has been compared by no less a person than General Sherman to a bent fishing-hook;…Monterey itself is cosily ensconced beside the barb. Thus the ancient capital of California faces across the bay, while the Pacific Ocean, though hidden by low hills and forest, bombards her left flank and rear with never-dying surf. In front of the town, the long line of sea-beach trends north and north-west, and then westward to enclose the bay. The waves which lap so quietly about the jetties of Monterey grow louder and larger in the distance; you can see the breakers leaping high and white by day; at night, the outline of the shore is traced in transparent silver by the moonlight and the flying foam; and from all round, even in quiet weather, the distant, thrilling roar of the Pacific hangs over the coast and the adjacent country like smoke above a battle.

~ Robert Louis Stevenson, *Across The Plains*, 1888

Scenic Monterey Peninsula. Pub. Bell Magazine Agency.

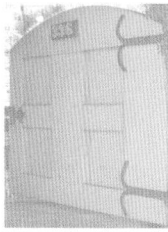

Introduction

Xue elo xonia euene. (I come from rock.)
~ Ohlone/Costanoan Esselen Nation

A ship has just docked in Monterey Bay. It is the 1800s and you are Monterey's newest resident. Are you ready to try your hand at the life of a settler in Monterey? Perhaps you are an entrepreneur looking for opportunities in this new town. In a few years you might be appointed mayor, start the first newspaper, build a town hall, leave for the gold mines or marry into a local family and become a ranchero.

Depending upon when you arrived in the 1800s there could be a Spanish, Mexican or American flag flying down at the harbor. At different times, Monterey belonged to all three countries. The name Monterey means King's Mountain from the Spanish.

The people of Monterey witnessed many dramatic changes during the 1800s. Some of these events include the dismantling of the Mission system, the opening of the West, the 1849 constitutional convention at Monterey, the admission of California into the Union as the thirty-first state in 1850, the gold rush and the shift from major port and whaling center to turn of the century tourist destination.

First hand accounts by General Fremont, W.T. Sherman, the first consul Thomas Larkin, John Steinbeck, Robert Louis Stevenson, travelers, gold speculators, and sailors compliment the photos of over forty historic structures and heritage gardens.

These humorous and poignant reminiscences are a celebration of the history of Monterey. Through them the footprints of Native Americans, explorers, missionaries, pioneers, gold speculators, entrepreneurs, bandits and sailors are ever visible.

…Contentment, and a love of the wild and beautiful, will construct its tabernacle among the flowers, the waving shades, and fragrant airs of Monterey. And even they who now drive the spade and drill in the mines, when their yellow pile shall fill the measure of their purposes, will come here to sprinkle these hills with the mansions and cottages of ease and refinement. Among these soaring crags the steps of youth will still spring, and beauty garland her tresses with wild-flowers in the mirror of the mountain stream.
~ Walter Colton, alcade, *Three Years in California*, 1850

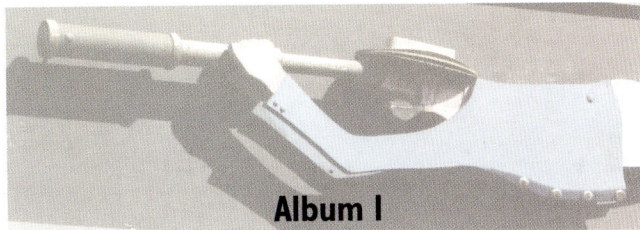

Album I

Along The Water

We came to anchor within two cable lengths of the shore, and the town lay directly before us, making a very pretty appearance; its houses being of whitewashed adobe, which gives a much better effect than those of Santa Barbara, which are mostly a mud color. The red tiles, too, on the roofs, contrasted well with the white sides and the extreme greenness of the lawn upon which the houses- about a hundred in number—were dotted about, here and there, irregularly. There are in this place, and in every other town, which I saw in California, no streets nor fences (except that here and there a small patch might be fenced in for a garden), so that the houses are placed at random upon the green. This, as they are of one story, and of the cottage form, gives them a pretty effect when seen from a little distance.
~ Richard Henry Dana, sailor, *Two Years Before The Mast*, a personal narrative, 1841

Custom House

...the cargo having been entered in due form, we began trading. Our cargo was an assorted one; that is, it consisted of everything under the sun. We had spirits of all kinds (sold by the cask), teas, coffee, sugars, spices, raisins, molasses, hardware, crockery-ware, tin-ware, cutlery, clothing of all kinds, boots and shoes from Lynn, calicoes and cotton from Lowell, crapes, silks; also, shawl, scarfs, necklaces, jewelry, and combs for the women; and, in fact, everything that can be imagined, from Chinese fireworks to English cart-wheels...
~ Richard Henry Dana, sailor, *Two Years Before The Mast*, a personal narrative, 1841

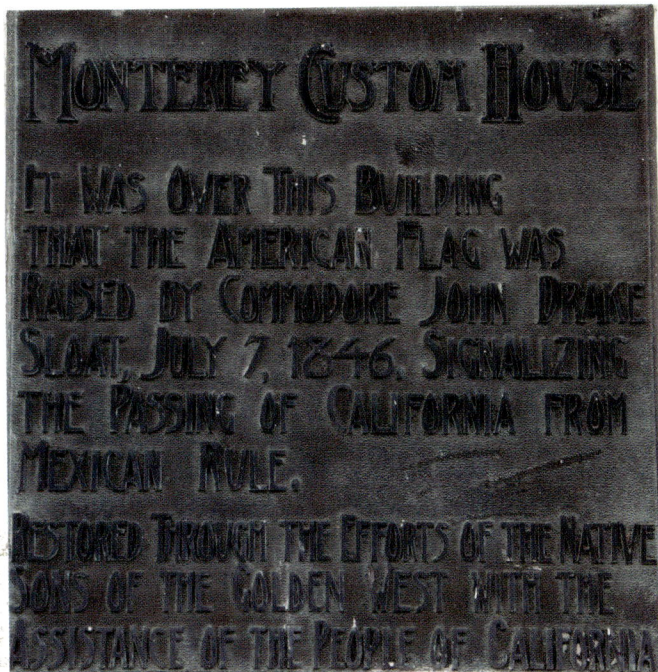

MONTEREY CUSTOM HOUSE

IT WAS OVER THIS BUILDING THAT THE AMERICAN FLAG WAS RAISED BY COMMODORE JOHN DRAKE SLOAT, JULY 7, 1846, SIGNALIZING THE PASSING OF CALIFORNIA FROM MEXICAN RULE.

RESTORED THROUGH THE EFFORTS OF THE NATIVE SONS OF THE GOLDEN WEST WITH THE ASSISTANCE OF THE PEOPLE OF CALIFORNIA

The Custom House is registered as California State Historical Landmark #1, a National Historical Landmark, and on the National Register for Historic Places.

Vintage 1940s postcard. Pub. Bell Magazine Agency. Old Custom House, Monterey.

In front of Custom House.

Side of the custom house with anchor. Custom House is located on Main and Decatur Streets. It might be the oldest public building in California with sections built as early as 1814. The central section was built in 1827 and later enlarged during 1841-46.

Detail of door.

The original custom house—there was no mistaking it, for it was founded on a rock-overhung the sea, while the waves broke gently as its base, and rows of sea-gulls sat solemnly on the skeletons of stranded whales scattered along the beach. A Captain Lambert dwelt on the first floor of the building; a goat fed in the large hall —it bore the complexion of a stable—where once the fashionable element tripped the light fantastic toe.

~ Charles Warren Stoddard,
In The Footprints of The Padres, 1902

Today the Custom House is a two story adobe with a long Monterey verandah, a top balcony with French doors, a wooden floor replacing the original dirt floor and a shake roof.

Custom House Garden

The small cactus garden by the Custom House is stocked with varieties of cacti gathered from the Southwest in the 1920s.

A large whaling pot.

Fisherman's Wharf

In an hour we steamed into a fog-bank, so dense that even the head-light of our ship was as a glowworm; and from that moment until we had come with in sound of voices on the undiscovered shore, it was all like and voyage in the clouds. Whistles-blew, bells rang, men shouted, and then we listened with hungry ears. A whistle answered us from shore—a piercing human whistle. Dim lights burned through the fog. We advanced with fearful caution; and while voices out of the air were greeting us, almost before we had got our reckoning, we drifted up under a dark pier, on which ghastly figures seemed to be floating to and fro, bidding us all-hail. And then and there the freedom of the city was extended to us, saturated with salt-sea mist. Probably six times in ten the voyager approaches Monterey in precisely this fashion.
~ Charles Warren Stoddard, *In The Footprints of The Padres*, 1902

Fisherman's Wharf is located off Del Monte Avenue. There are two wharfs in fact, Fisherman's Wharf and Wharf #2. The harbor of Monterey was a hub of activity during the 1800's.

A view of the wharf in the distance. The original wharf was a stone pier extending from the Customs House, which was then under Mexican control. Vessels moored and unloaded goods on the docks after their long trip around Cape Horn. Customers, sailors and businessmen would gather on the dock to check out the latest arrivals. As the fishing industry grew in Monterey a second wharf was built.

The stores along the wharf. In 1870 Pacific Coast Steamship Company constructed the wharf for passenger and freight service. By 1913 the wharf was no longer run privately but by the city of Monterey. This change in control corresponded with the growth of the local sardine industry. The wharf has seen numerous modernizations mirroring its transformation from working wharf to tourist attraction.

A candy store where Salt Water Taffy is made before your eyes. The pink candy-cane striped awning and the sugary smell wafting out the door draw the crowds in.

A sailor on the lookout.

A seafarer in front of a popular wharf restaurant.

A friendly pelican.

Now as we lay off Monterey,
The boys began to frisk-O!
And some did swear, is wind was fair,
We'd soon be at Francisco.
Drops large and small, in many a squall,
And now and then a spray too,
O'er head and feet were sure to meet
And that both night and day too.
From various hands the pots and pans
Disperse in every quarter,
Some salt junk eat, while others treat,
And never mind the water.
One thing we know, that we can show,
And that to without boasting,
We've all enough of this 'ere stuff
Called California coasting.
And thus we talk and act, but then
'Tis useless so to hanker,
These things well bear, 'till all is fair,
And then run in and anchor.
~ Octavius Thorndike Howe, *Argonauts*
of Forty-Nine, History & Adventures of the
Emigrants (1849-50), 1923

Houseboat for year-round living on the water.

The Star of Monterey. Whale watching tours are a popular excursion. The Grey Whales migrate from December to April and from May to November humpback and blue whales can be seen in outer Monterey Bay. You might also see dolphins, porpoises, sea lions and sea otters.

Monterey Fishing Company. The nearby Municipal Wharf II built in 1926 is home to several wholesale fish companies and a commercial abalone farm. A 700-foot fishing promenade extends from the wharf- no license is required and anyone may fish from the East side of the Wharf. Pods of sea lions gather around the pier or nearby docks. From here it is a good 30-minute walk or 5-minute drive to Cannery Row.

11

Whaling Station

There is a whaling station here, employing a large number of red and green boats, which are all carefully placed under sheds, evidently to keep them from accidentally getting wet. This fact, together with a singular absence of the far-reaching odor peculiar to oil-boiling localities, induced us to interrogate a piratical –looking chap. In a red cap and long boots, who was carefully sharpening a harpoon on a grindstone…. "Look here, my man, did you ever really see a whale in your life?…The intrepid harpooner scratched his head…" Well, between you and I, stranger, I never did. I wouldn't get into one of them dern boats for a fortune. The fact is, we are just hired by the railroad ad hotel company to stand around and make believe.

~ Derrick Dodd (pseudonym Frank Harrison Gassaway),
Summer Sauntering, semi-humorous letters
for the *San Francisco Evening Post.* 1882.
A great example of 'early tourism' in Monterey!

The Whaling Station is located at 391 Decatur Street in Heritage Harbor. This is a view of the Whaling House from the footbridge to the Presidio. David Wright built the home in 1847 but left a few years later in 1849 for the gold fields.

The building was the site of the first off shore whaling operation in Monterey. The Old Portuguese Whaling Company used this home for it's on shore activities from 1855.

A detail of the sidewalk.

A whaler's pot.

The only whaling sidewalk left in Monterey.

Whaling Station and First Brick House Garden

The home is now leased by the Junior League of Monterey County who rent out the Whaling House and its gardens for weddings and other events. The garden lies between the historic Whaling Station and the First Brick House.

Detail of a bench outside the backdoor of the Whaling Station, which affords a quiet spot to gaze at the garden. A chalk rock wall frames the garden.

Cannery Row

Cannery Row in Monterey California is a poem, a stink, a grating noise a quality of light, a tone, a habit, a nostalgia, a dream. Cannery Row is the gathered and scattered, tin and iron and rust and splintered wood, chipped pavement and weedy lots and junk heaps, sardine canneries of corrugated iron, honky-tonks, restaurants and whore-houses, and little crowded groceries and laboratories and flop-houses.

~ John Steinbeck, *Prologue to Cannery Row*, 1945

The Monterey Aquarium is located at 886 Cannery Row. The aquarium is a great place to begin a walking tour of Cannery Row. The aquarium was once the Hovden Cannery. Built by Knut Hovden, an innovator in cannery technology, in 1916. It was the largest and oldest cannery in Monterey. Now a few benches sit in front of the massive boilers once the heart of the operation. The aquarium has over 300,000 marine plants and animals and opened in 1984

The Outer Bay Wing was added in 1996 doubling the exhibit space. The exterior decks provide panoramic views of the ocean.

Bust of John Steinbeck at the beginning of Cannery Row. The bronze bust of Steinbeck gazes directly across Cannery Row at the Steinbeck Centre. Behind is the Steinbeck Plaza, a shopping complex. Cannery row runs parallel to the Monterey shoreline. The street is the closest one to the water.

The Wing Chong building is located at 835 Cannery Row, the market and it's owner appeared in Steinbeck's Cannery Row. In fact the first character in chapter one is Lee Chong of Lee Chong's Heavenly Flower Grocery Store. The building dates to 1918. There is a small Steinbeck museum containing newspaper clippings and photos in the store.

The crowds at Cannery Row. Immortalized by Steinbeck in his trilogy of books, Cannery Row (1945). Tortilla Flat (1935) and Sweet Thursday the place has taken on mythic proportions. Cannery Row's original name was Ocean View Boulevard. It was originally a wagon rutted dirt road made famous by John Steinbeck. The street was officially renamed in 1958 in honor of Steinbeck. At the time the books were written it was lined with sardine canneries, shacks, bars and flophouses. Flash-forward to 2008, tourist stores, high-end wine tasting bars, a world-class aquarium and shopping centers dominate the strip and of course, hotels.

Monterey Canning Company

Early morning is a time of magic in Cannery Row. In the gray time after the light has come and before the sun has risen, the Row seems to hang suspended out of time in a silvery light. The streetlights go out and the weeds are a brilliant green. The corrugated iron of the canneries glows with the pearly lucence of platinum or old pewter. No automobiles are running then. The street is silent of progress and business. And the rush and drag of the waves can be heard as they splash in among the piles of the canneries. It is a time of great peace, a deserted time, a little era of rest.

~ John Steinbeck, *Cannery Row*, 1945

There were originally sixteen crossovers on Cannery Row. The Monterey Canning Co. walkover is the only original one left. Walkovers were used to carry canned fish from the factory to the warehouse. The Monterey fishing industry began in the mid-1800s when Chinese fishing families arrived. Later on Japanese fisherman arrived to fish for salmon and then the row would be home to Sicilian immigrants. Today, tour buses fill the streets and the Wave Trolley ferries tourists and Steinbeck's pilgrims back and forth along the strip. Long gone are Mack and now in their place are the curious tourists.

The Cannery Row Company walkover. In the early 20th century, sardines were plentiful in Monterey earning it the title 'sardine capital of the world.' Unfortunately due to over fishing the sardine population declined and by the 1950s most canneries had closed.

The Monterey Bay Coastal Trail runs from Pacific Grove to Castroville. A section of the trail runs through Cannery Row and provides the visitor to Monterey with a fun alternative to the tour bus. During the summer months the four-wheel surreys are the choice vehicles of transportation.

15

Maritime Museum

One day, all the inhabitants of the town rushed together in a crowd to the port, to witness the arrival of a huge steamer which had appeared in the offing; the largest that had passed along this coast and, as I understood, the first into the bargain. The Californians gazed at it in silent wonderment, not at all able to comprehend how it could have been constructed of such a size; how it could be made to go without sails; where all the smoke it cast out of its huge funnel came from; and how the large fire in its inside did not burn the vessel up. She was the California, the first of the new American line steamers; and, having cast anchor and landed her passengers,...

~ William Redmond Ryan, traveler, *Personal Adventures in Upper and Lower California*, 1848-9

The museum is located at 5 Custom House Plaza. With over 6000 artifacts, 50,000 photographs and 6,000 books the museum is a must for fans of maritime history. Children will love the giant rotating lens from the Point Sur Lighthouse.

Detail of anchor. The museum is located at the site where Commodore John Sloat claimed Monterey for the United States

The cactus garden in front of the museum.

The fountain in the main courtyard.

Album 2

In The Town

Alvarado Adobe

The lethargic little town of Monterey is the quaintest place we have visited since Santa Fe. It is one of the towns where we have to rouse ourselves occasionally to make sure we are not dreaming. The locality was first "discovered' in 1602, when Vizcaino landed here and took possession of the country in the name of Phillip III of Spain, naming it in honor of the Viceroy of Mexico, Gaspar de Zuniga, Count of Monterey, who was projector of this Northern cruise. Over 160 years later, still prior to our birth as a nation, the hitherto unbroken silence of this primitive region was stirred by another inscription on history's page, the founding of the Old Carmel Mission by Father Serra, president of the band of Franciscan missionaries. ...Many of Monterey's residents are still of Spanish blood and their homes bear that distinctive national type, many being built of adobe and in some instances surrounded by high walls, which roses clamber over. The old one-story Spanish theatre still stands, though now used as a storehouse.
~ Susie C. Clark, traveler, *The Round Trip from Hub to the Golden Gate*, 1890

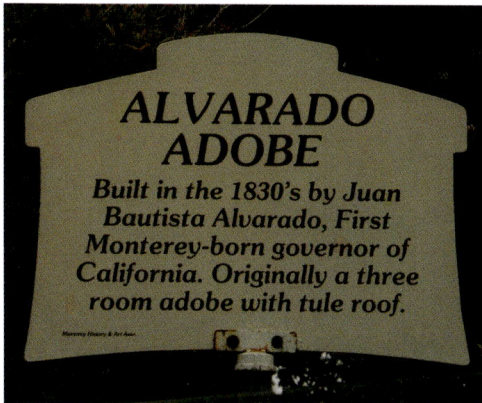

ALVARADO ADOBE

Built in the 1830's by Juan Bautista Alvarado, First Monterey-born governor of California. Originally a three room adobe with tule roof.

The Alvarado adobe is located at 510 Dutra Street.

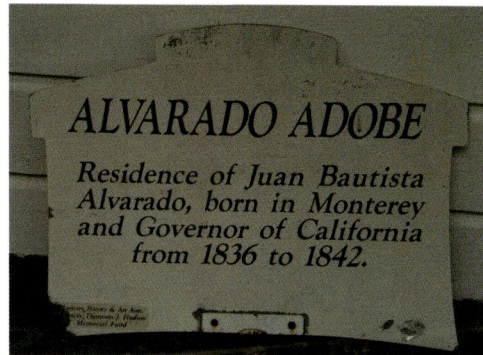

ALVARADO ADOBE

Residence of Juan Bautista Alvarado, born in Monterey and Governor of California from 1836 to 1842.

Don Juan Bautista Alvarado, the first Monterey-born Governor of Alta California, built the home in the 1830s. The home was later purchased by Manuel Dutra in 1842 and remained in the family until 1946.

The adobe includes a Monterey-style covered verandah, shake roof and long windows adorned with black shutters.

This view shows the plantings in front of the home and an addition made to the original three room adobe sometime in the past.

California's First Theatre

I was not ready to go to the mines till the latter part of July, and when I did, after buying two horses, I went alone, for the bulk of the people who were going to the mines had left; and if women's rights had come to the vote then I suppose they would have carried the day, as there was three women left in the town to one man.
~ J. Swan, editor John A. Hussey, *A Trip to the Gold Mines of California,* 1848

First California Theatre. Pub. Bell Magazine Agency.

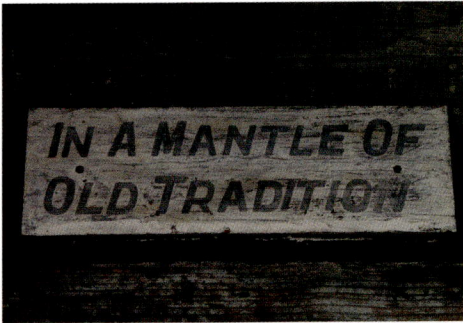

One of two signs above the main entrance.

The theatre is located on the southwest corner of Scott and Pacific streets. The First Theatre is registered California State Historical Landmark #136. Jack Swan, an English sailor who arrived in Monterey in 1843, built it in 1844. The building operated as a saloon and a boarding house. Jack Swan caught gold fever like many other residents of Monterey and left in 1848 only to return later.

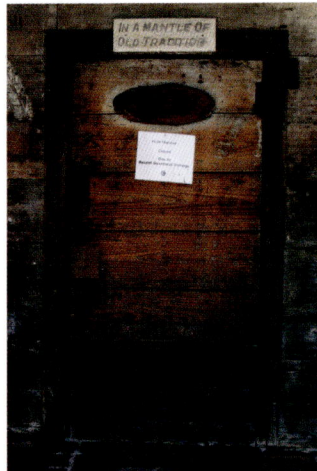

The main entrance into the theatre from Pacific Street. In 1848 discharged soldiers of the 1st New York Volunteers put on minstrel shows and dramatic performances.

A view of the front porch. The Troupers of the Gold Coast once again revived the role of theatre in the 1930s. Over 2000 actors have preformed at the theatre since 1937.

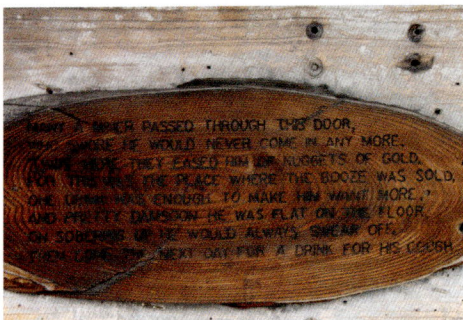

The First Theatre has a past as interesting as any of the plays performed over the decades. It has been a tearoom, curio shop, museum, bookstore, the headquarters of a whaling company, and a theatre. This is one of two signs above the main entrance.

Many a miner passed though this door who swore he would never come in any more. Twas here they eased him of nuggets of gold.
For this was the place where the booze was sold.
One drink was enough to make him want more and pretty dam soon he was flat on the floor.
On sobering up he would always swear off.
Then come in next day for a drink for his cough

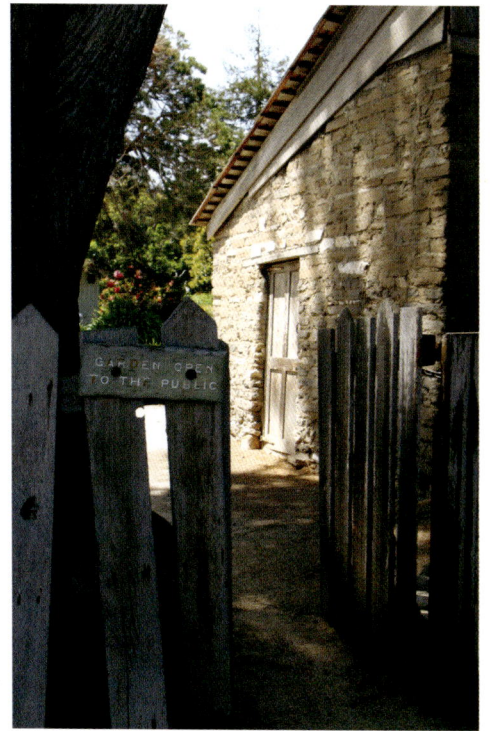

The theatre is located at the Southwest corner of Pacific and Scott Streets. The price of one admission ticket on opening night was $5.00. The first plays staged at the theatre included "Putman, the Iron Son of '76", "Cox and Box" and "Nan, the Good-for-Nothing."

The garden was laid out in the 1920s. The Historic Garden League and the staff of the California State Parks maintain the garden.

The Hearst Foundation donated the First Theatre to the Sate of California.

A building probably used for storage behind the theatre.

The barracks attached to the theatre.

A lookout station from which sailors could see whaling ships in port.

California's First Theatre Garden

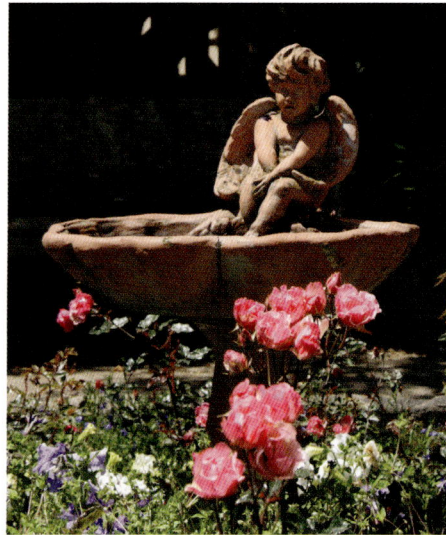
A detail of the birdbath.

The theatre is currently closed due to a branch falling from the giant sequoia in the back garden.

A quiet garden with winding paths, tucked in behind the theatre.

Capitular Hall

*The blacksmith dropped his hammer, the carpenter his plane, the mason his trowel, the farmer
his sickle, the baker his loaf, and the tapster his bottle. All were off for the mines…*
~ Walter Colton, alcade, *Three Years in California*, 1850

Capitular Hall is located on the corner of Pacific and Franklin
Streets. Guy Freeman Fling of Sonora built it in 1834. It was
originally a one-story building.

Over the years it has changed, a second story was added and the front
porch removed. It may have been an early town hall.

The building is presently used by the Monterey Institute of
International Studies.

The entrance way onto Franklin Street.

Casa Abrego

Senor Abrego, who is of Mexican origin, was the most industrious Californian I saw in the country. Within a few years he had amassed a large fortune, which was in no danger of decreasing. I attended an evening party at his house, which was as lively and agreeable as any occasion of the kind could be. There was a tolerable piano in his little parlor, on which a lady from Sydney, Australia played "Non piu mesta". Two American gentlemen gave us a few choice flute duets, and the entertainment closed by a quadrille and polka, in which little son of Senor Abrego figured, to the general admiration.

~ Bayard Taylor, *Eldorado or Adventures in the Path of Empire Writer*, 1850

CASA ABREGO
Señor Jose Abrego constructed this adobe structure in 1834

Casa Abrego sign is located at 592 Abrego Street. Don Jose Abrego, a Spanish merchant, built the home. He came to Monterey from Mexico in 1834.

Don Jose Abrego acted as Treasurer of Alta California until American occupation in July 1846.

A view of the home looking South up Abrego Street.

Today, the Casa Abrego has a gray shake roof with long narrow French doors opening onto the verandah.

Casa Abrego's brick courtyard on the North side of the building.

Casa Alvarado

This quaint old town was the former county seat of Monterey county. It is handsomely situated upon the southern part of the bay of the same name; has nearly or quite four thousand inhabitants, and is one of the most wonderfully contrived collections of houses to be seen this side of Mexico. If the buildings had been dropped down from the moon, one house at a time, it could not present a more deranged conglomeration. They are mostly of the old Spanish style, the material adobe, the shape long, low and porched, and plastered upon the outside; white in color, with tiled roofs, and little prism like windows set in the thick walls with iron bars...

~ Caroline M. Churchill, *Over The Purple Hills, or Sketches of travel in California, embracing all the important points usually visited by tourists,* 1881

Casa Alvarado is registered as California Landmark # 348. The home is located at 494-498 Alvarado St. Governor Alvarado who served from December 20, 1836 to December 20, 1842 built it.

A long narrow French door with iron balustrade.

At the time Casa Alvarado was completed, it and the Larkin home were the only two-story homes in Monterey.

Casa Amesti

Observing a card upon one of the numerous doors, announcing To Let, or For Sale, I wondered if this referred to one compartment or the whole long row. There is no regularity in the streets. In some places the thoroughfare must continue alongside of a house very straight, then its course is interrupted by a three cornered structure standing just where the road should continue; the consequences is, there is a branching off each side of the impediment, and an angle taken in some unexpected direction. A few buildings stand protruding cornerwise into the street. One comes to the conclusion that every man caused his lot to face which way it best pleased him, and that no two fronts consecutively in one direction a few gardens are enclosed with a wall of stone five or six feet in height.

~ Caroline M. Churchill, *Over The Purple Hills, or Sketches of travel in California, embracing all the important points usually visited by tourists, 1881*

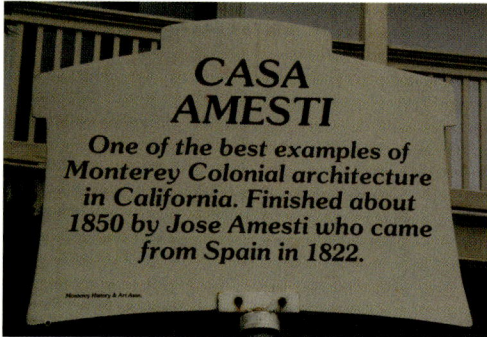

Casa Amesti is located at 516 Polk Street.

Don Jose Amesti, a Spaniard from the Basque region, built the home between 1833-1850s. The two-story adobe is an example of Monterey Colonial architecture.

Looking North on Polk Street. Casa Amesti was left to the National Trust for Historic Preservation.

The famed interior designer Frances Adler Elkins also resided at Casa Amesti. She made additions to the home and restored it in 1919. The Casa Amesti is a two-story adobe with a shake roof, long narrow windows and formal clipped hedges in the front. Elkin's brother David Adler designed the formal walled gardens.

The front entrance on Polk Street.

Casa Bonifacio Site

Monterey. It is situated on the bay of that name, and is connected with Salinas, its successful rival for the county seat, by a narrow-gauge railroad seventeen miles long. I went over with my sick boy, and we stayed during the evening and over night there. ...It is beautifully located in a long sloping cove in the mountains, which are yet covered with majestic pines. Its outlook on the bay, the entrance to which is 20 miles road, is magnificent, and it well deserved the name of the "Mountain of the King." It has a good wharf, and plenty of water of 2,500 tons burden.
~ D.L. Phillips, *Letters From California: its mountains, valleys, plains, lakes, rivers, climate and productions. Also its railroads, cities, towns and people, as seen in 1876*, 1876

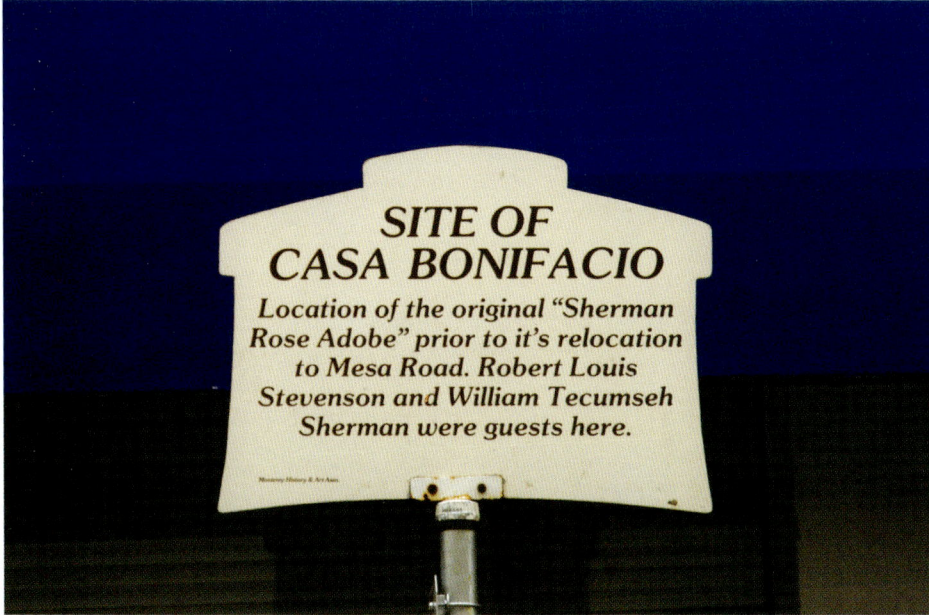

SITE OF CASA BONIFACIO

Location of the original "Sherman Rose Adobe" prior to it's relocation to Mesa Road. Robert Louis Stevenson and William Tecumseh Sherman were guests here.

Monterey History & Art Assn.

Only the sign remains of the Casa Bonifacio built in 1835 by Jose Rafael Gonzales, the administrator of the Custom House. The house was moved to Mesa Road in 1922 to make way for a bank. A romantic Monterey legend has it that the subsequent owners daughter Maria Ygnacia was betrothed to Lt. William T. Sherman. He gave her a rose and promised to return to marry her but he never did. Another version has Lt. W. T Sherman planting a rose bush before he leaves and telling the girl that when it blooms he will return. The bush that grew here was called the Sherman Rose.

Photo taken before 1922. A view of Original Adobe in original location. Library of Congress, Prints and Photographs Division, Historic American Buildings Survey or Historic American Engineering Record, Reproduction Number HABS, CAL, 27-MONT, 30-1

Casa Buelna

The curving line of the Bay of Monterey is nearly duplicated by the mountain range 20 miles inland, and in this pleasant sunny strip of territory, Santa Cruz is situated. It is a quiet seacoast town, with pretty residences and gardens, and attractive shops, which display shells, delicate mosses, and their treasures of the sea. There are two miles of beautiful beach within the city limits, and in the cliffs beyond, the first sculptor, Neptune has carved grottoes and natural bridges, which richly reward a drive thither…

~ Susie C. Clark, traveler, *The Round Trip From The Hub To The Golden Gate*, 1890

Don Antonio Buelna built the casa in 1820. The first school for girls in Monterey was located here. Casa Buelna is now a private residence. Recently it sold for more than two million dollars. The adobe is situated on just over two acres of land, with rose gardens, a separate cottage and even tennis courts. The home is located at 801 Masa Road.

Casa De La Torre

Incidents of a Walk to Monterey. I stayed but four or five days in San Francisco on my return. The Convention, elected to form a constitution for California, was then in session at Monterey, and partly as an experiment, partly for economy's sake, I determined to make the journey of one hundred and thirty miles on foot. Pedestrianism in California, however, as I learned by this little experience, is something more of a task than in most countries, one being obliged to carry his hotel with him. The least possible bedding is a Mexican sarape, which makes a burdensome addition to a knapsack, and loaf of bread and flask of water are inconvenient, when the mercury stands at 90. Besides, the necessity of pushing forward many miles to reach " grass and water" at night, is not very pleasant to the foot-sore and weary traveler. A mule, with all his satanic propensities, is sometimes a very convenient animal.

~ Bayard Taylor, Eldorado or Adventures in the path of empire: comprising a voyage to California, via Panama; life in San Francisco and Monterey

CASA
DE LA TORRE
Built for Don Jose
Joaquin de la Torre,
alcalde of old Monterey.

Monterey History & Art Assn.

Casa de la Torre is located at 502 Pierce Street. The Alcade of Monterey Philip Roach granted the property to Francisco Pico in c.1850. The original adobe had three rooms but over time several additions were made.

Today, the adobe includes, a tile and shake roof, Monterey-style verandah, double sash windows with green shutters and a beautiful garden out front.

Pink rose bushes set off the white washed walls of the adobe.

Looking Northwards on Pierce Street.

This large window on the North wall is a more recent renovation.

A classic long verandah.

A detail of the clay and shingle roofs.

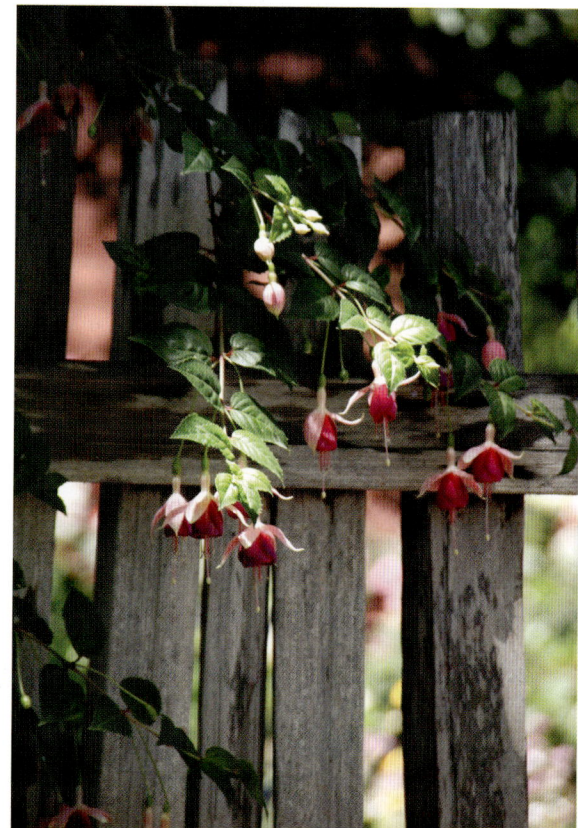

A detail of one of the blooms in the side garden.

Casa del Oro

It took me till 2 pm next day to reach Monterey, for I could buy no feed for the horse at Blanco's, and I had to stop on the road to let the horse feed. When I arrived in Monterey one of the soldiers offered me $16 for the horse, poor as he was. And I sold him, and he took him up to the fort, and though he was pretty weak for a while, plenty of Uncle Sam's hay and barley put him on good order, and when he went on furlough next spring to the mines, he took the horse with him and sold him there for ten ounces of gold—not a bad speculation as it cost nothing to feed the horse while in Monterey.
~ Jack Swan, A Trip To The Gold Mines Of California In 1848

Casa del Oro is registered as California Landmark #532. It is located in the Custom House Plaza, on the corner of Scott and Olivier Streets. The home was built c.1843 and originally used as a barracks.

A view of the Casa del Oro looking up towards the Duarte Store and Cole House. The building became a general store run by Joseph Boston in the 1850s. The name 'Casa Del Oro' may come from a time when the building was used as a saloon and later as a gold dust exchange for miners. The casa is a two-story adobe with white washed walls, a tiled roof and four windows on the front.

Joseph Boston's store contained the only free-standing safe in Monterey. David Jacks bought the building in 1855 and his daughters restored and donated the building to the State.

Casa del Oro Herb Garden

Blooms by Picket Fence garden shop. There are three gardens located in this area. In the plaza in front of the Picket Fence is the Sensory Garden, beside the store is the Herb Garden and beyond is the Casa Del Oro Garden located at the corner of Pacific and Scott Streets in Monterey.

A view of the Sensory garden looking towards Pacific House and Memory Garden.

A bench inside the garden next to the gift shop run by the nonprofit Historic Garden League.

A detail of the herb garden. The beds are edged with clay tiles. The herb garden lies between the Sensory Garden and the newer Casa del Oro garden..

A view of the Casa Del Oro garden looking towards the oldest theatre. The Casa del Oro garden is located at the corner of Pacific and Scott Streets. The garden was once the site of a parking lot, now beautifully transformed by the Historic Garden League, in conjunction with the State Historic Park.

Blooms in the garden.

Crows enjoying breakfast in the Casa Del Oro garden

The fountain beckons tourists into the garden and is located on the upper most terrace, closest to the First Theatre.

31

Casa Estrada

After breakfast G. and myself went on shore, on a visit to the Commandant, Don Marian Estrada, whose residence stood in the central part of the town, in the usual route from the beach to the Presidio. It was built of adobe—brick...it was not displeasing; for the outer walls had been plastered and whitewashed giving it a cheerful and inviting aspect. Our Don was standing at his door; and as we approached, he sailed forth to meet us with true Castilian courtesy, shook me cordially by the hand, then bowed us ceremoniously into the sala. Here we seated ourselves upon a sofa at his right. During conversation cigarritos passed freely; and, although thus early in the day, a Proffer was made of refreshments.
~ "Captain Robinson's Life in California," 1829, as printed by Charles Warren Stoddard,
~ *In The Footprints of The Padres*, 1902

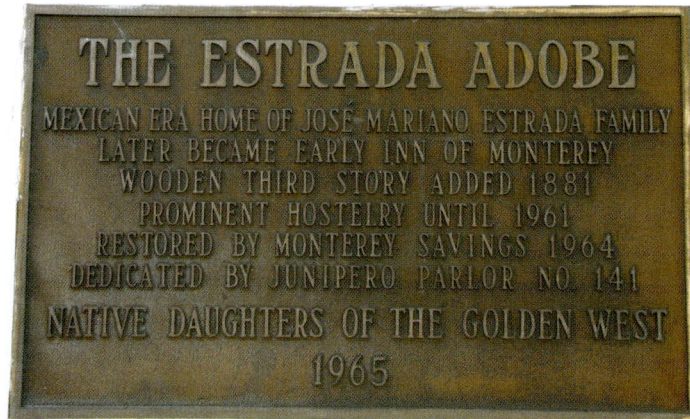

THE ESTRADA ADOBE
MEXICAN ERA HOME OF JOSÉ MARIANO ESTRADA FAMILY
LATER BECAME EARLY INN OF MONTEREY
WOODEN THIRD STORY ADDED 1881
PROMINENT HOSTELRY UNTIL 1961
RESTORED BY MONTEREY SAVINGS 1964
DEDICATED BY JUNIPERO PARLOR NO. 141
NATIVE DAUGHTERS OF THE GOLDEN WEST
1965

The Casa Estrada is located at 470 Tyler Street. Don Jose Mariano Estrada built the casa in 1823. Jose Mariano Estrada was a civil and military official.

The Casa Estrada is located at 470 Tyler Street. Don Jose Mariano Estrada built the casa in 1823. Jose Mariano Estrada was a civil and military official.

Today the Casa Estrada consists of two floors, an upper verandah with balustrade, long narrow windows and a shake roof.

Casa Gutierrez

I have never been in a community that rivals Monterey in its Spirit of hospitality and generous regard. Such is the welcome to the privileges of the private hearth, that a public hotel has never been able to maintain itself. You are not expected to wait for a particular invitation, but to come without the slightest ceremony, make yourself entirely at home, and tarry as long as it suits your inclination, be it for a day or for a month. You create no flutter in the family, awaken no apologies, and are greeted every morning with the same bright smile. It's not a smile which flits over the countenance, and passes away like a flake of moon-light over a marble tablet. It is the steady sunshine of the soul within. If a stranger, you are not expected to bring a formal letter of introduction. No one here thinks any better of a man who carries the credentials of his character and standing in his pocket. A word or an allusion to recognized persons or places is sufficient.
~ Walter Colton, alcade, *Three Years in California*, 1850

Casa Gutierrez is registered as California State Historical Landmark #713. It is located at 590 Calle Principal. Don Joaquin Gutierrez, the Governor of Alta California for a mere three months, built the house in 1836.

CASA GUTIERREZ
Built in the Mexican period

The two-story adobe has been a residence, an art gallery, a restaurant and now the offices for State Senator Abel Maldondo. The home at one time had an additional wing, later torn down.

A detail of the door facing onto Calle Principal.

Casa Munras

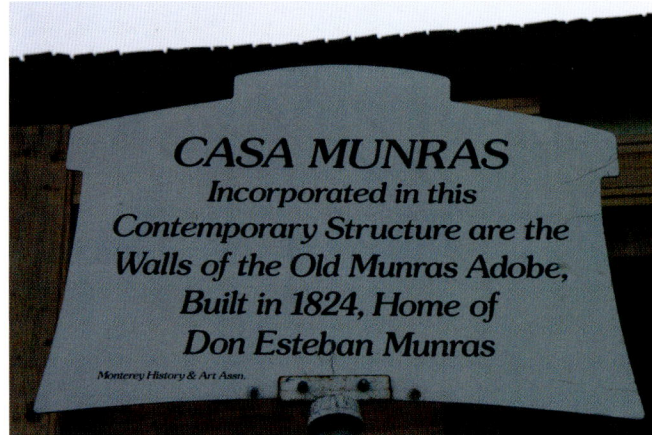

CASA MUNRAS
*Incorporated in this
Contemporary Structure are the
Walls of the Old Munras Adobe,
Built in 1824, Home of
Don Esteban Munras*

Monterey History & Art Assn.

Casa Munras is located at 700 Munras Avenue. In the early 1800s most Monterey homes were being constructed within the safety of the walls of the Royal Presidio. Casa Munras was one of the first buildings to be constructed outside.

The last Spanish diplomat to California, Don Esteban Munras, built a home in 1824. Don Esteban's great granddaughter, Maria A. Field sold the home in 1941 to JP Dougherty who converted it into a hotel. *Note: Casa Munras was under construction when this book was assembled.*

Casa Pacheco

Sir, I have rec'd on your a/c. two hundred Dollars worth of very in deferent looking Soap. I have heard you talk much about your very Superior Soap, but had known the kind you was going to send me, and how long a time I was to wait, I would not have trusted you one hundred dollars. You have now owed me a long time, and say you owe me only Soap, (when I say you also owe me hides,) and appear to think you will send me only Soap and that when ever you see fit. After keeping me waiting so long, you now send me only 200$ worth of Soap and that very dirty. Your next excuse I suppose will be that its a dry season and you will have no tallow. You must remember you told me 3 or 4 times that you had all your soap ready for cutting so the dry season can make no difference. In conclusion I have to say I do not intend to write any more to you for my own, and if you receive a letter from the Alcalde to appear in Monterey this month you must blame yourself and not me.

~ Letter to Francisco Pacheo from Thomas Larkin, threatening him with legal action, April, 1843. The Larkin Papers, Vol. 2, p.14.

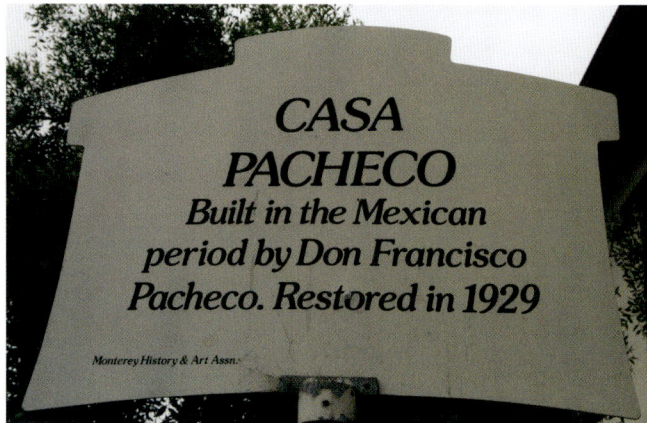

Casa Pacheo is located on Abrego Street. Don Francisco Pacheco built the casa in 1840. Don Francisco Pacheco came to Monterey in 1820. He was part of the Spanish army and a carriage maker. Later he became the treasurer of Monterey and in 1833 acquired his first ranch land from the Mexican government

The building has been altered over the years and is now home to a social club.

The entrance onto Abrego Street. Casa Pacheco was also used as a boarding house and a hospital.

Casa Sanchez

She boasted but half a dozen thinly populated streets. One might pass through these streets almost any day, at almost any hour of the day, footing it all the way from the dismantled foil on the seaside to the ancient cemetery, grown to seed, at the other extremity of the settlement, and not meet half a score of people. Geese fed in the gutters, and hissed as I passed by; cows grazing by the wayside eyed me in grave surprise; overhead, the snow-white sea-gulls wheeled and cried peevishly; and on the heights that shelter the ex-capital the pine-trees moaned, and often caught the seafog among their branches, when the little town was basking in the sunshine and dreaming its endless dream. How did a man kill time in those days? There was a studio on Alvarado street; it stood close to the Post-office, in what may be generously denominated as the busiest part of the town. The studio was the focus of life and hope and love; some work was also supposed to be done there. It was the headquarters of the idle and the hungry, and the seeker after consolation in all its varied forms.
~ Charles Warren Stoddard, *In The Footprints of The Padres*, 1902

Casa Sanchez is located at 414 Alvarado Street. It was built in the 1820s. A customs official called Gil Sanchez once lived in the adobe. Later he was a founder of Santa Clara College. The original building was a one-story home with a verandah running along the length of the rear.

CASA SANCHEZ
Part of the former residence of
Dona Maria Ignacia Sanchez.
The garden extended through
to Calle Principal

In the past Casa Sanchez was used as a police station, tea room and beauty parlor.

The building is currently used as a bar. The two-story adobe has an upper verandah with narrow French doors and a shingled roof,

Casa Serrano

The one common note of all this country is the haunting presence of the ocean. A great faint sound of breakers follows you high up into the inland canons; the roar of water dwells in the clean, empty rooms of Monterey as in a shell upon the chimney; go where you will, you have but to pause and listen to the voice of the Pacific.

~ Robert Louis Stevenson, *Across The Plains*, 1879

CASA SERRANO
Built by Don Florencio Serrano, an Alcalde in old Monterey

Monterey History & Art Assn.
Courtesy Thomas J. Hudson
Memorial Fund

Casa Serrano is located on 412 Pacific Street.

It was built by Don Florencio Serrano, the second mayor of Monterey under American rule in the 1840s.

The home became one of the first Californian schools. The Monterey History and Art Association restored the home in 1959. Today Casa Serrano is a single story adobe with a shake roof, a long Monterey style verandah and formal clipped bushes in front.

Casa Serrano Garden

Casa Serrano has a lovely brick courtyard with a multitude of blooms viewable from a side stairway leading up towards Pierce Street.

The picket fence with daisies running along the East side of the home.

Casa Soberanes

No one can be in Monterey a single night, without being startled and awed by the deep, solemn crashes of the surf as it breaks along the shore. There is no continuous roar of the plunging waves, as we hear on the Atlantic seaboard; the slow, regular swells—quiet pulsations of the great Pacific's heart-roll inward in unbroken lines and fall with single grand crashes, with intervals of dead silence between. They may be heard through the day, if one listens, like a solemn undertone to all the shallow noises of the town, but at midnight, when all else is still, those successive shocks fall upon the ear with a sensation of inexpressible solemnity. All the air, from the pine forests to the sea, is filled with a light tremor and the intermitting beats of sound are strong enough to jar a delicate ear.

~ Bayard Taylor, writer for *The New York Tribune, Eldorado or Adventures in the path of Empire*, 1849

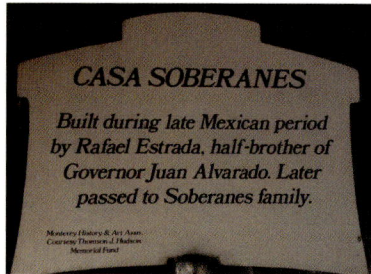

CASA SOBERANES

Built during late Mexican period by Rafael Estrada, half-brother of Governor Juan Alvarado. Later passed to Soberanes family.

Monterey History & Art Assn.
Courtesy Thomson J Hudson
Memorial Fund

Casa Soberanes is registered as California State Historical Landmark #712. The home is located at 336 Pacific Street.

Members of the Soberanes family lived in the House with the Blue Gate from 1860 until 1922.

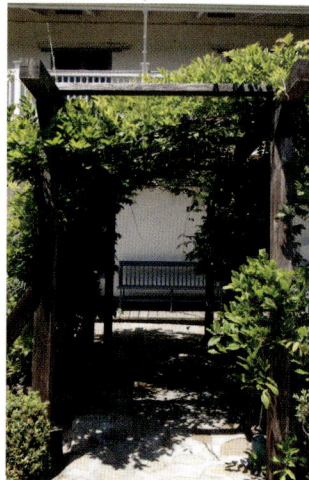

The home's nickname is 'the house with the blue gate.' Casa Soberanes is a two-story Mexican adobe. Inside the home are objects from New England as well as Modern Mexican folk art. Built in the 1830s by Don Jose Estrada and later sold to Don Feliciano Soberanes family in 1860.

The arbor in front of the home. The sala would have opened onto the verandah in the front.

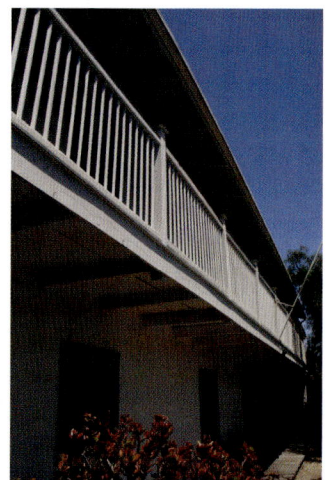

Detail of upper balcony. It is possible to slightly make out a staircase, which once led from the south corner of the verandah.

Casa Sobranes Garden

The grape vine at the back of the home is said to have been planted by Ezequiel Jr. Front, gardener at the Carmel mission who retained the property for a period of time.

Detail of doorknocker.

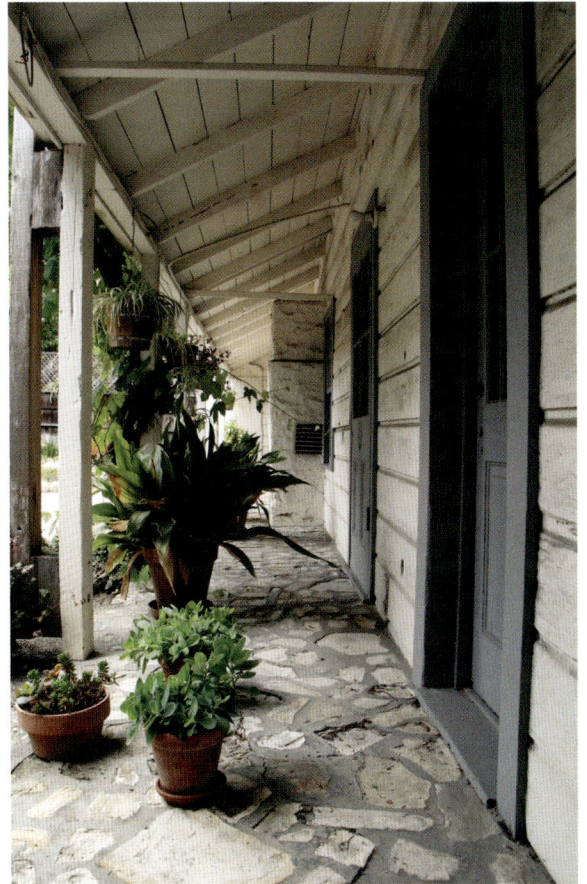

The Casa Soberanes garden was originally planted in the 1920s.

Local historian Mayo Hayes-O'Donnell gave the property to the State of California in 1953.

The back of home showing the porch and roof.

Detail of a cherub.

A welcoming chair invites the passerby to sit and admire the beauty behind the blue gate

A garden view.

Birdbath and foliage.

More garden with birdbath in center.

California poppies.

Examples of different materials used to etch the garden beds. Here abalone shells are used.

Green glass wine bottles used to highlight a bed.

Whale bone harks back to Monterey's past.

Cypress tunnel along side of the home. The cypress trees have helped the casa by keeping pollutants at bay and also act as a sound barrier.

The tiled roofs are a great curiosity to persons not accustomed to seeing them. The tiles are of a light brick or cinnamon color, and look like long earthen flower pots, split in two lengthwise, or like a length or red earthen stove pipe (if one can imagine such a thing), and the split it lengthwise. The lower row placed with concave side upwards, the upper row with concave side downwards, forming little troughs for carrying off the water. ...In fact these tiles suggest the idea of huge rolls of cinnamon bark placed upon the roof to cure.

~ Caroline M. Churchill, traveler. *Over The Purple Hills or Sketches of travel in California embracing all the important points usually visited by tourists,* 1881

41

Colton Hall

The town-hall, on which I have been at work for more than a year, is at last finished. It is built of white stone, quarried from a neighboring hill, and which easily takes the shape you desire. The lower apartments are for school; the hall over them –seventy feet by thirty—is for public assemblies. The front is ornamented with a portico, which you enter from the hall. It is not an edifice that would attract any attention among public buildings in the United States; but in California it is without rival. It has been erected out of the slender proceeds of town lots, the labor of the convicts, taxes on liquor shops, and fines on gamblers. The scheme was regarded with incredulity by many; but the building is finished, and the citizens have assembled in it, and christened it after my name, which will now go down to posterity with the odor of gamblers, convicts, and tipplers.

~ Walter Colton, alcade, *Three Years in California,* 1850

Colton Hall is registered California State Historical Landmark #126.

Everybody knew that the convention was about closing...The citizens, therefore, as well as the members, were in an excited mood. Monterey never before looked so bright, so happy, so full of pleasant expectations.

~ Bayard Taylor. *Eldorado or adventured in the path of empire,* 1850. Taylor was a writer and during the summer of 1849 he worked for the *New York Tribune* as a special correspondent to California.

A 1940s postcard of Colton Hall. Pub. Bell Magazine.

Colton Hall was erected in 1849 by the Reverend Walter Colton the chief administrator of Monterey. It was designed to be both a school and a town hall. It became the first capital of California. Rev. Colton was influential in Monterey for establishing California's first newspaper in 1846, *The Californian*. Walter Colton and Robert Baylor Semple co-published *The Californian*.

Colton Hall Garden

I saw numbers of little people all about town, but there was no school for them. I talked with Ex-Alcade Walter Colton about it. ... He said that many of the people would be only too glad to send their children to school, and pay tuition, if anybody would teach them. "Very well," I said, " Give me a room in Colton Hall and send them along. I'll teach them, at any rate for a while." The children came, some forty or fifty boys and girls. They did not know English, and I did not know a word of Spanish. We got together any number of stray primers and alphabets, and picture books, and spelling books, and so forth, and with the help of the blackboard, we got on after a fashion. I kept on for six months, till in September the Constitutional Convention came along, and wanted Colton Hall to meeting; and so my school had to surrender.
~ S.H. Willey, *Thirty Years in California: a contribution to the history of the state from 1849 to 1879*

The second floor of the building is a re-creation of when California's first Constitution was drafted in October 1849.

A welcoming bench amongst the blooms of Colton Hall.

The bronze Seal of California.

Sesquicentennial Plaques

The bronze plaques highlight important events in Monterey
history from early times to statehood in 1850 and beyond.

These plaques recalling significant dates in Monterey's history were installed to commemorate the Sesquicentennial of the California State Constitutional Convention, held in Colton Hall between September 1, 1849 and October 13, 1849, when the constitution was signed

City of Monterey
City Council
Colton Hall Museum and Cultural Arts Commission
Dedicated October 13, 1999

1602
PORT OF MONTEREY NAMED
Sebastian Vizcaíno, a Spanish explorer, anchors in the bay and names it Monterey in honor of Gaspar de Zuniga y Azevedo, the Count de Monte Rey, Viceroy of New Spain and sponsor of the expedition.

THE ANCIENT ONES
Native Americans of this region lived in Monterey for thousands of years before Spanish explorers arrived in California.

1770
SPANISH EXPEDITION CLAIMS MONTEREY
Captain Don Gasper de Portolá reaches Monterey on his second land expedition. Father Junipero Serra arrives by ship. Together they claim Monterey for Spain and establish the Mission and Presidio of San Carlos Borromeo de Monterey.

1542
FIRST RECORDED SIGHTING OF MONTEREY BAY
Juan Rodriguez Cabríllo, a Portuguese navigator sailing for Spain, sights Monterey and names it "Baia de los Pinos," Bay of the Pines.

1775
SPANISH CAPITAL MOVES TO MONTEREY
The provincial capital moves from Loreto, Mexico to Monterey.

1776

ARRIVAL OF DE ANZA EXPEDITION

After a 2,200-mile trek from Tubac, Mexico
leading 240 colonists, Captain Juan Bautista de Anza
arrives in Monterey.

1818

MONTEREY CAPTURED

During the Spanish-American wars of independence,
Hippolyte de Bouchard, a Frenchman commanding an
Argentinean privateer, lands and captures Monterey,
driving the Spanish defenders inland. After ransacking
the town, Bouchard and his men sail down the coast
continuing their attacks at several ports.

1793-94

EL CASTILLO

A Spanish military fortification is constructed
on an ancient Native American village site
overlooking Monterey's harbor.

1822

THE HIDE AND TALLOW TRADE

Ships from Boston begin arriving to purchase hides, often called
"California banknotes", and tallow from the missions and ranchos.
Two Years Before the Mast by
Richard Henry Dana leaves us a grand description of this trade.

1794

ROYAL PRESIDIO CHAPEL

The oldest building in Monterey, this is now
the San Carlos Cathedral.

1804

CALIFORNIA DIVIDED

Alta California is divided from Baja California and
Monterey is named the capital of Alta California; it
remains under Spanish jurisdiction.

1822

MEXICAN INDEPENDENCE FROM SPAIN

California acknowledges Mexico's independence from Spain, which was declared in 1821. Monterey remains capital of Alta California under Mexican rule.

1828

PORT OF ENTRY

Monterey is designated as the only port of entry for Alta California. All foreign ships must have their cargoes inspected at the Custom House and pay import taxes.

1827

A MOUNTAIN MAN JAILED IN MONTEREY

Jedediah Strong Smith, a mountain man and beaver trapper, opened the first American overland route to California in 1826. The following year the Mexican government jailed him in Monterey because they thought he was a spy.

1842

CALIFORNIA MISTAKENLY CLAIMED FOR THE UNITED STATES

Believing that the United States is at war with Mexico, Commodore Thomas ap Catesby Jones, Commander of the American Pacific Squadron, captures Monterey and claims California for the United States. When he discovers this is a mistake, he apologizes and sails away.

1827

CUSTOM HOUSE

One portion of this building was constructed by the Mexican government for the collection of duties from foreign shipping. After the United States takes California, the American government expands the building and operates it as a United States Customs House until 1867. It is the oldest U.S. government building in California.

1846

AMERICAN FLAG RAISED AT MONTEREY

With the outbreak of hostilities with Mexico, Commodore John Drake Sloat, as commander of the Pacific fleet, raises the American flag at the Custom House and declares California a part of the United States.

1846

FIRST NEWSPAPER IN CALIFORNIA IS ESTABLISHED IN MONTEREY

Robert Semple, participant in the Bear Flag Revolt and later President of the California Constitutional Convention, and Walter Colton, Alcalde of Monterey, establish the first newspaper in California, *The Californian*.

1849

CALIFORNIA STATE CONSTITUTIONAL CONVENTION

Colton Hall serves as the site of the first California constitutional convention. Forty-eight delegates from ten districts in California debate for six weeks to create the state's first constitution. This constitution was written in both Spanish and English.

1848

GOLD DISCOVERED

News of the discovery of gold at Coloma reaches Monterey. Many people depart for the gold fields, leaving Monterey almost abandoned.

1849

FIRST PUBLIC LIBRARY IN CALIFORNIA IS ESTABLISHED IN MONTEREY

1849

FIRST POST OFFICE IN CALIFORNIA ESTABLISHED AT MONTEREY

The Pacific mail steamer, "California" arrived in Monterey on February 24, 1849. This exciting event brought the first mail to the first post office in California.

1849

COLTON HALL COMPLETED

Walter Colton, Alcalde of Monterey, completes the construction of Colton Hall with the aid of taxes on rum, fines for gambling, and the labor of jailed offenders. It will be used as a public assembly hall and school.

1850
STATEHOOD

California is admitted to the United States as the 31st state. The constitutional convention of 1849 designated San Jose as the first state capital.

1851
Chinese Fisherman

Chinese immigrants arrived in Monterey and created the area's first commercial fishing trade. By using techniques imported from China the innovative fishermen developed a dried-fish market which capitalized on the growing Chinese population in California and the exporting of dried fish to China.

1850
City Government

On March 30, 1850, by special act of the State Legislature, it was proclaimed that "lands heretofore known and acknowledged as the Pueblo of Monterey shall henceforth be known as the City of Monterey."

1854
Monterey Shore Whalers

Captain J.P. Davenport organized the first shore whaling company which was followed in 1855 by seventeen Portugese fishermen who started the "Old Company." Between 1854 and 1888, over 95,000 barrels of whale oil were produced from Monterey Bay whales.

1770-1870
A City of Women

Monterey's women of all nationalities gathered and while doing wash provided a medium for information through the "Wash Tub Mail" at Washer Woman's Gulch. It was Monterey's women who kept the town's business and commerce alive when most of the men left for the gold fields.

1859
City Lands Sold

David Jacks acquired 30,000 acres of City of Monterey lands for $1,002.50 and became the most prosperous land baron in the city's history. He was immortalized not with a statue but through Jacks Peak, Jacks Park and Monterey Jack Cheese.

1850 - 1880
Emporium of the Valleys

Between 1850-1880 Monterey was a commercial port and known as the "Emporium of the Salinas and Carmel Valleys." In 1869, the Pacific Steamship Company completed a "good and substantial wharf."

1875
Italian Fishermen

Italian fishermen arrived in Monterey and joined the Chinese in harvesting fresh fish for shipment throughout California via the Monterey and Salinas Valley Railroad. This new and important culture helped transform Monterey's fresh-fish Industry.

1874
Monterey's First Railroad

The Monterey and Salinas Valley Railroad was constructed as a narrow-gauge, granger railroad linking Monterey to the rest of California. For the first time, Monterey was easily reached by land bringing hope to Monterey's new destiny.

1879
Robert Louis Stevenson

In poor health, almost penniless and with his literary success still a few years away, Robert Louis Stevenson created a romantic view of Monterey and the surrounding area. His written and mental notes of the Monterey coastline were later used when he wrote "Treasure Island," "Kidnapped" and "The Old Pacific Capital."

1874
Bohemian Monterey

World renowned artist Jules Tavernier established a studio in Monterey. A bohemian culture soon followed as Monterey became a favorite ocean-side retreat for artists and writers.

1880
Hotel Del Monte

Charles Crocker utilized the Southern Pacific Railroad Company's construction arm, the Pacific Improvement Company, to rebuild Monterey's rail service and to construct a grand hotel to exploit the beauty of Monterey Bay. The Hotel Del Monte galvanized Monterey into a world-class tourist destination. Today the former hotel and its grounds are part of the Naval Postgraduate School.

Cooper Molera Complex

The old town of Monterey was once the most hospitable and agreeable town in the State. Thirty years ago it could boast of lots of pretty girls of refinement and education, and the jolliest lot of men and women that were ever congregated together. Now, to us pioneers, it looks terribly lonesome, and the less we see of it the better we feel, for the town is decay, personified, and not agreeable to contemplate for those who know that they themselves have passed the summit, and are on the shady side of life's journey. As long as Don David Spense and the good Don Juan Cooper remained of the old crowd of long ago, the place was tolerable, their hospitality was a sunlight in itself, that made things look cheerful, but since they have passed away there is a chill in all the surroundings, that Davy Jacks, who now owns the whole town, and, they say, "has it fenced in," finds it impossible to dispel.

~ William Grey, *A Picture of Pioneer Times in California, Illustrate with Anecdotes and Stories Taken from Real Life.* 1881

The Cooper Molera complex is located at 508 Munras Street. John Cooper, the half brother of Thomas Larkin began construction on the home in 1834.

Window detail.

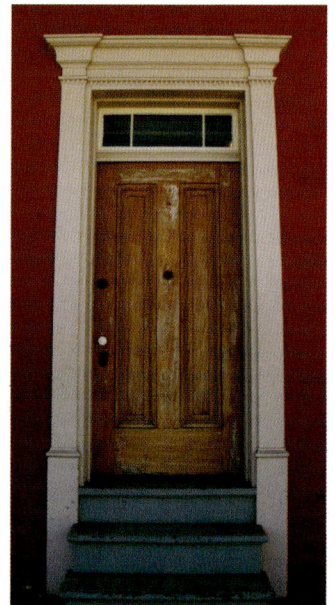

John Cooper married Encarnacion from a local prominent family.

The building was changed from a simple adobe style into a town house complete with Victorian dining room in the 1850s.

Side of the store.

View towards the home.

View towards the home.

Cooper Molera Garden

The sheep and chicken pen by the Eastern wall.

One of three Minorca chickens, which wander the property. The chickens like the blooms are historically accurate as their ancestors were introduced to California in the early days of settlement.

The Cooper barn.

The barn doors.

Inside the barn is a display of beautiful carriages and paper decorations.

The herb garden by the Cooper Museum is filled with herbs essential to a home in the 1800s.

The large outdoor oven.

A wooden bench to view the garden.

All the plantings in the garden were based on plant lists introduced to California before 1865, the year John Cooper and his wife, Encarnacion, left Monterey for San Francisco. Frances Grate is credited with extensively researching and re-creating the period garden behind the Cooper-Molera complex.

More blooms in this historic period garden.

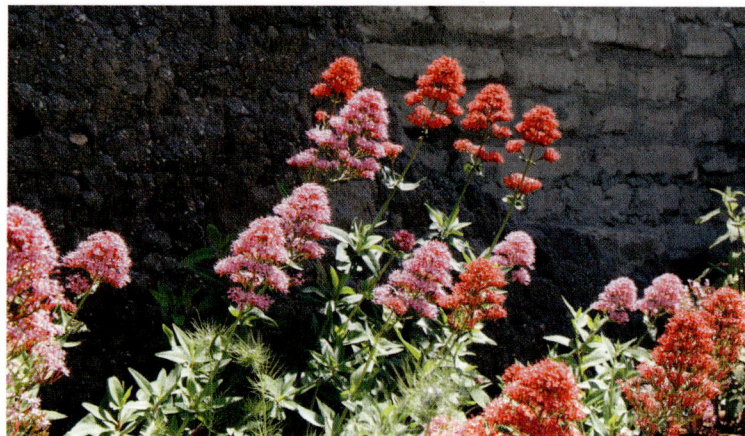

Blooms along the outer stone wall.

Doud House

The great, overshadowing, determining question at the outset was: Shall the State be a free State, or a slave State? The preponderance of sentiment in favor of a free State was so great that it was one of the earliest matters determined; and it was settled almost without debate, and with not a vote recorded against freedom.
~ S.H. Willey, Presbyterian Minister, Thirty Years in California; a contribution to the history of the state from 1849 to 1879.

The home is located at 177 Van Buren Street. Francis Doud built the home in the 1850s. It is a great example of a wooden home from the early American Period. Look for the four Monterey cypress trees planted by the Douds. Francis Doud was the Sergeant of Arms for California Constitutional Convention of 1849.

The Monterey History and Art Association acquired the home in 1969. The one story adobe has unobstructed views of Monterey Bay.

Doud House Garden

Here is a partial view of the knot-garden. Florence Yoch, a landscape architect, designed a portion of the garden. Florence Yoch is perhaps best known for designing the sets for Gone With the Wind and Romeo and Juliet with partner Lucile Council.

Duarte's Store

Another thing that surprised me was the quantity of silver in circulation. I never, in my life, saw so much silver at one time, as during the week that we were at Monterey. The truth is, they have no credit system, no banks, and no way of investing money but in cattle. Besides silver, they have no circulating medium but hides, which the sailors call "California banknotes."
~ Richard Henry Dana, sailor, *Two Years Before The Mast*, a personal narrative, 1841

Duarte's Store is located at 220 Olivier Street. The building was moved from 120 Main Street.

The building is thought to have been constructed by Rosario Duarte who operated a store from this building. The building is dated to c.1865. The Duarte store operated as a general store. Today the building is used as a restaurant.

El Cuartel Site

Major Smith, who was Paymaster for the stations of Monterey and San Diego, had arrived only a few days previous, from the latter place. He was installed in a spacious room in the upper story of the cuartel, which by an impromptu partition of muslin, was divided into an office and bedroom. Two or three empty freight-boxes, furnished as a great favor by the Quarter Master, served as desk, table and wash-stand. There were just three chairs for the Major, his brother and myself, so that when we had a visit, one of us took his seat on a box. The only bedding I brought from San Francisco was a sarape, which was insufficient, but with some persuasion we obtained a soldiers pallet and an armful of straw, out of which we made a comfortable bed.

~ Bayard Taylor, correspondent for *The New York Tribune*, *Eldorado or Adventure in the Path of Empire*, 1849, published in 1850

SITE OF EL CUARTEL
A long two-story adobe which served as barracks for soldiers and headquarters for the Mexican Government in the 1840's.

Monterey History & Art Assn.

Only a sign remains of the massive two-story adobe, which once stood here. The El Cuartel provided quarters for up to 50 soldiers making up Monterey garrison. The offices of the Governor and other official were located here as well. The first library was housed in El Cuartel, a Mexican government building built in 1840. The building was destroyed in 1910. Originally the Mexican army barracks but later used by US forces in 1846. The Californian, the first newspaper and even the first library and the first public school in Monterey used the building.

A view of El Cuartel from the Historic American Buildings Survey O'Donnell Collection Monterey, California ca. 189 HABS CA,27-MONT, 31-1.

First Brick House

Prior to the year 1845, that great domain lying west of the Rocky Mountains and extending to the Pacific Ocean was practically unknown. About that time, however, the spirit of inquiry was awakening. The powerful voice of Senator Thomas H. Benton was heard both in public address and in the halls of Congress, calling attention to Oregon and California. Captain John C. Fremont's famous topographical report and maps had been accepted by Congress, and ten thousand copies ordered to be printed and distributed to the people throughout the United States. The commercial world was not slow to appreciate the value of those distant and hitherto unfrequented harbors. Tales of the equable climate and marvelous fertility of the soil spread rapidly, and it followed that before the close of 1845, pioneers on the western frontier of our ever expanding republic were preparing to open a wagon route to the Pacific coast.
~ Eliza P. Donner Hougton, *The Expedition of the Donner Party and its Tragic Fate*

Gallant Duncan Dickenson of Virginia built the house in 1847. The Dickensons were one of the survivors of the ill-fated Donner party. This is a view of the home from the South West.

The Dickensons departed Monterey in 1848 for the gold rush.

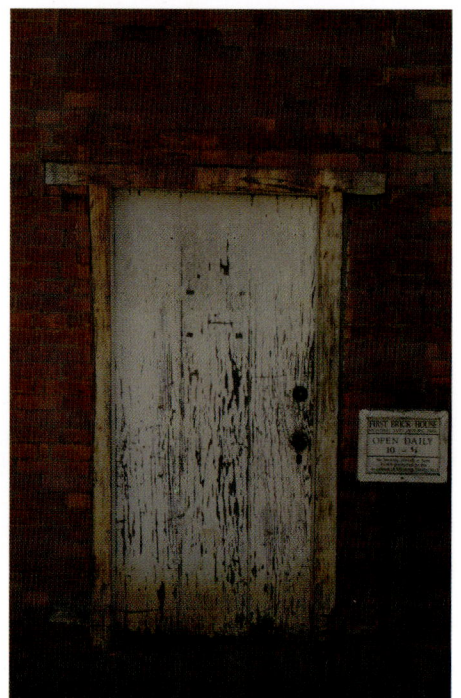

The house has been used as a private residence and even a Spanish restaurant.

The First Brick House is a simple building of fired brick. A staircase, which once led to the second story, has been removed.

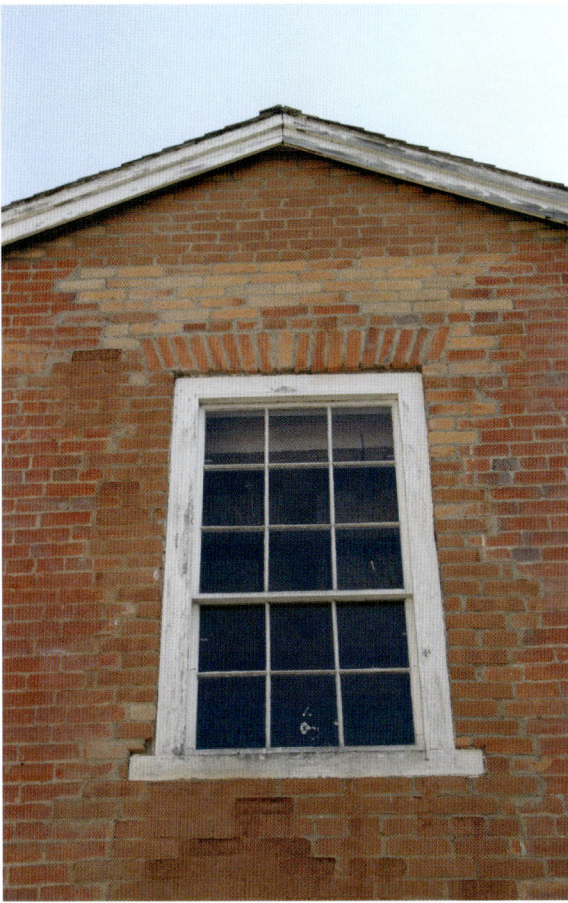

The First Brick House is located at 351 Decatur Street.

The left wall of the Brick House with a few plantings.

A view of the chimney at the back of the house looking towards Decatur Street.

A detail of the side door.

Fremont Adobe

Among the California ladies were some married to Americans, and they came at once to see me; others, who were thoroughly California, and to whom my name represented only invasion and defeat, did not come at first, but after a little were among the kindest people I knew there. The only cow in town belonged to one of these, and she sent me daily a portion of the milk because I too had a little child.
~ Jessie Benton Fremont, wife of explorer and later Senator John Charles Fremont, *A Year of American Travel*, 1878

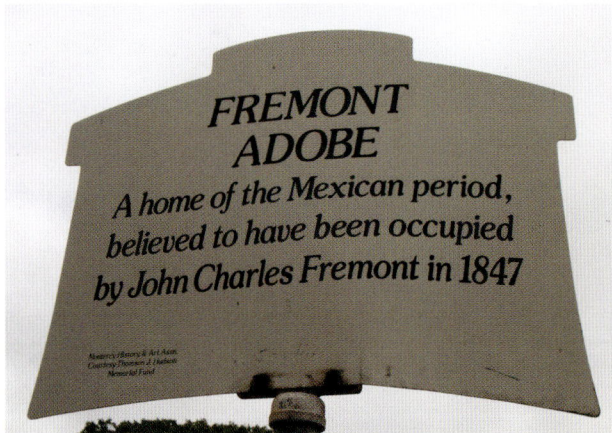

The Fremont adobe is located at 539 Hartnell Street.

A simple adobe from the Mexican Period. It was thought to be the home of Lt. John C. Fremont of the Army Topographical Corps who came to Monterey in 1846. He was known as "The Pathfinder of The Rocky Mountains."

A simple adobe from the Mexican Period. It was thought to be the home of Lt. John C. Fremont of the Army Topographical Corps who came to Monterey in 1846. He was known as "The Path-finder of The Rocky Mountains."

John C. Fremont was the first candidate of the United States Republican Party for the office of President of the United States.

First French Consulate

The emigration from all parts of the Americas to this place is still increasing day by day. Over ten thousand people from Sonora and Lower California men, women and children, have passed within a few leagues of Monterey during the last two months, and more keep coming. Most of the emigrants from those countries who come by land travel on burros (mulets) and bring more or less provisions with them, but many others make this long and wearisome journey on foot and are so poor and so destitute that they have to beg along the way for their food. Among those who come on the ships there are also many who arrive here without the slightest resources, having in many cases sold all they had to pay their passage. All of these people find themselves in great difficulty when they get here. When they arrive in the ports they are still far from the gold.
~ Jacques Antoine Morenhout, French Consul to Monterey, May 15, 1849,
as published in *The Inside Story of the Gold Rush*, 1935

The First French Consulate is located at 404 Camino El Estero. The French Consulate was originally located at Franklin Street and Estero. It was later restored and moved to its new location beside Lake El Estero.

The first French Consul to Mexican California lived here. The home has been a private residence and headquarters for the Girl Scouts. Today, the Monterey visitor centre is located here.

The French Consulate is a one story adobe with shake roof and a long verandah on the back.

Gabriel de la Torre Adobe

A romantic glamour overhangs the region. Before the Declaration of Independence was framed, this portion of California had been settled by Spanish missionaries; and the missions and churches which they founded remain, many of them intact, and are still the places of worship; others have yielded to the touch of "time's effacing finger," and are piles of ruins. Wherever the sites of these churches and missions are found, however, they present objects of profound interest; not only because of their venerable antiquity, but as indicating the intelligent foresight of their founders.

~ Major Ben C. Truman, newspaper correspondent, *Semi-tropical California; its climate, healthfulness, productiveness, and scenery,* 1874

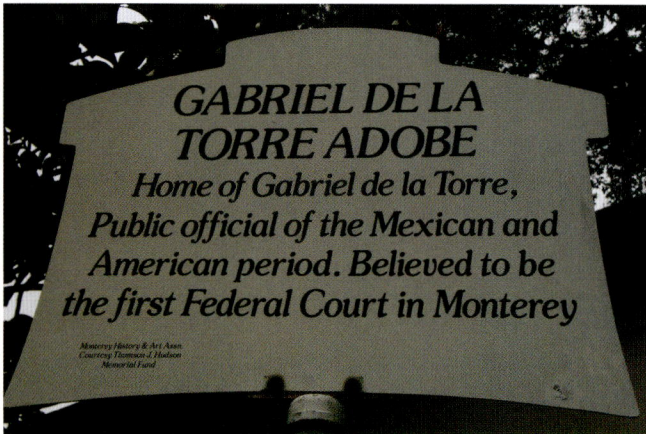

GABRIEL DE LA TORRE ADOBE
Home of Gabriel de la Torre, Public official of the Mexican and American period. Believed to be the first Federal Court in Monterey

Monterey History & Art Assn.
Courtesy Thomas J. Hudson
Memorial Fund

Gabriel de la Torre Adobe is located at 599 Polk Street.

The home was built c.1832 by Don Jose de la Torre a Mexican Alcalde. It was used as a Federal Court in 1834 first under Mexican rule and later under American possession in 1846.

For many years it was known as The Green Adobe where owner Nellie Smith ran a bookstore and tearoom.

A detail of the main door on Polk Street.

General Sherman's Quarters

The department headquarters still remained at Monterey, but, with the few soldiers, we had next to nothing to do....The season was unusually rainy and severe, but we passed the time with the usual round of dances and parties. ...As was usual, the army officers celebrated the 22nd of February with a grand ball, given in the new stone school-house, which Alcade Walter Colton had built. It was the largest and best hall then in California. The ball was really a handsome affair and we kept it up nearly all night.

~ General William T. Sherman, *Recollections of California 1846-1861*,
as published in 1945

The adobe is located at 464 Calle Principal.

Thomas Larkin built this one room adobe in 1834.

General Sherman's Horse. Historic American Buildings Survey HABS CAL, 27-MONT, 8-1

The Sherman Adobe is a modest adobe with a shake roof, a single door on the rear, a double sash window with shutters and a solid door on the front.

General Sherman occupied the adobe from 1847 to 1849.

SITE OF
CASA BONIFACIO

*Location of the original "Sherman
Rose Adobe" prior to it's relocation
to Mesa Road. Robert Louis
Stevenson and William Tecumseh
Sherman were guests here.*

The back of the adobe taken from the Cooper-Molera complex.

*The barracks is a ruin, the piazzas hang about it like rotten cobwebs,
and no one answers the roll call there but the owl.*
~ Thomas Chard, traveler, *California Sketches*, 1888

Golden State Theatre

GOLDEN STATE THEATRE

Built in 1926 and designed by Reid Bros., architects of many California landmarks, this theatre was the first to show talking pictures on the Monterey Peninsula beginning in 1929.

Monterey History & Art Assn.

The Golden State Theatre is located at 417 Alvarado Street.

When the theatre opened in the late summer of 1926 it was the largest theatre between San Francisco and Los Angeles.

A Detail of the marquee. In 2007, diverse artists such as KD Lang and Leon Russell, to films such as Jaws or Jurassic Park could be seen here.

The theatre was designed by the San Francisco Bay Area firm the Reid Brothers

Gordon House

Emigrants from the United States are still pouring into the rich valley of the Sacramento. A letter from one of them says;--' It may not be uninteresting to you to know that the emigrants by land the present season far exceed the expectation of the most sanguine. No less than two thousand are now in the interior, and within a hundred miles of the settlements. They bring with them a large amount of intelligence, wealth, and industry, all of which are greatly needed in their new home. The Mormons alone have a train of more than three hundred wagons." These emigrants will change the face of California. We shall soon have not only the fruits of nature, but of human industry. We shall soon be able to get a ball of butter without churning it on the back of a wild colt; and a potatoe without weighing it as if it were a doubloon.

~ Walter Colton, alcade, *Three Years in California*, 1850

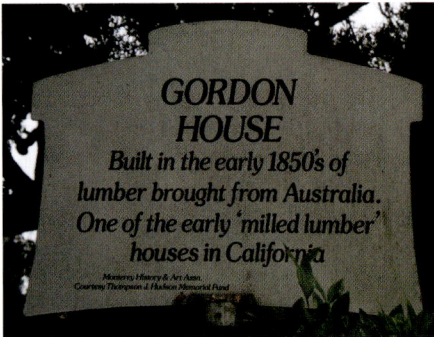

GORDON
HOUSE
Built in the early 1850's of
lumber brought from Australia.
One of the early 'milled lumber'
houses in California

Monterey History & Art Assn.
Courtesy Thompson J. Hudson Memorial Fund

Gordon House is located at 526 Pierce Street. This home was prefabricated and imported to Monterey in 1849 by Philip Roach. Philip Roach was the last alcade of Monterey.

The home is a one-story adobe with shake roof and long front verandah.

The home is named later Samuel Gordon who bought the home in 1871 and lived in it for 29 years.

A view of the verandah from the west side of the building.

A detail of the verandah and baluster.

House of Four Winds

How long this gathering of gold by the handful will continue here, or the future effect it will have on California, I cannot say. Three-fourths of the houses in the town on the bay of San Francisco are deserted. Houses are sold at the price of the ground lots. The effects are this week showing themselves in Monterey. Almost every house I hired out is given up. Every blacksmith, carpenter, and lawyer is leaving; brick-yards, saw-mills and ranches are left perfectly alone.

~ Thomas O. Larkin, Monterey, California, June 28, 1848

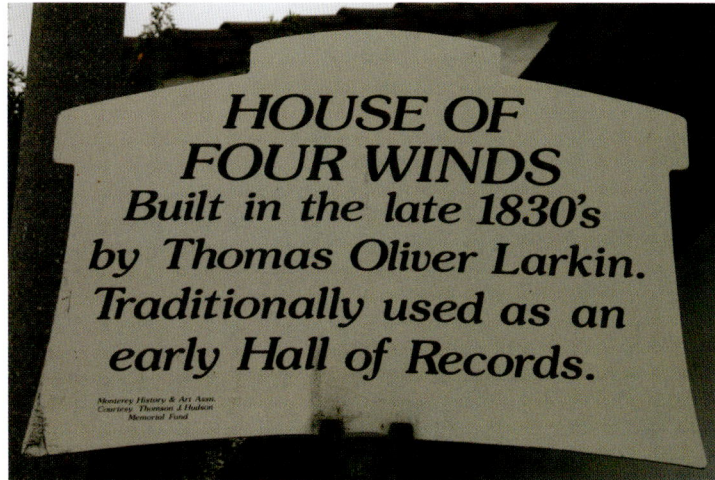

HOUSE OF
FOUR WINDS
Built in the late 1830's
by Thomas Oliver Larkin.
Traditionally used as an
early Hall of Records.

Monterey History & Art Assn.
Courtesy Thomson & Hudson
Memorial Fund

The House of The Four Winds is located on 540 Calle Principal. It was used as a residence by Governor Alvarada and as a store. The House of Four Winds is registered California State Historical Landmark #353.

Front view of La Casa de Los Quatro Vientos. The house is named for the weather-vane, one of the first to have such an adornment and for its roof that slopes in four ways. It was one of the first homes in Monterey to boost such an adornment. This adobe, built by Thomas Larkin in 1834, became the first state Hall of records. The Hall of Records was later moved to El Cuartel.

The women's civic club of Monterey bought the home in 1914 and turned it into a meeting house.

67

La Mirada Adobe Museum of Art

It seemed fitting after the noise and bustle of the great, wide-awake city of San Francisco that we should seek the quiet of Monterey, and amid the beauty, seclusion and sylvan loveliness of Hotel del Monte once more enjoy Nature in her fairest mood. Fortunately for us, the autumnal rains had ceased when we reached California in November, as we reveled in the benefits there of …Hotel del Monte, in its fine grove of cedar, oak, and pine, the loveliest spot on our continent, is garden-like in appearance and park-like in extent. There are nearly two hundred acres under cultivation, and upon them is employed a force of sixty men, who keep the flowerbeds, walks and turf in the highest state of order and perfection…Flowers in exquisite designs meet you at every turn, and all a mass of harmonizing yet contrasting colors. Great trees, whose bare trunks are entwined with ivy, sweet pea, wisteria, nasturtium and cobaea, raise their proud heads and bid defiance to the storm.

~ Mary H. Wills, *A Winter in California*

MONTEREY MUSEUM OF ART
LA MIRADA
CASTRO ADOBE
FRANK WORK ESTATE
720 VIA MIRADA

La Mirada is an art museum dedicated to artists of California and the Pacific Rim. Exhibitions focus on California and the Pacific Rim.

The home is a two-story adobe with tile roof, long verandah and land-scaped gardens.

The museum is located in one Monterey's oldest neighborhoods.

A heron by the pond behind the museum. The museum is surrounded by beautiful gardens.

Lara-Soto Adobe

These cypresses are quite instinct with individual life and quite as fantastic as any that Dore drew for his "Inferno." They are as gnarled and twisted as olive-trees two centuries old, their attitudes seem not only to show struggle with the elements, but agony in that struggle. The agony may be that of torture in the tempest, or of some fabled creatures fleeing and pursued, stretching out their long arms in terror, and fixed in that withering fear. They are creatures of the sea quite as much as of the land, and they give to this lovely coast a strange charm and fascination.

~ Charles Dudley Warner, journalist, *Our Ital,* 1890

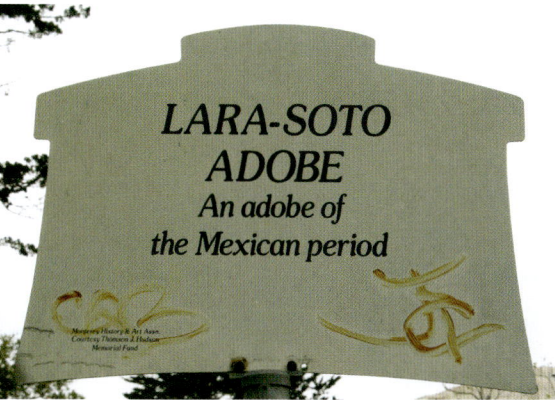

LARA-SOTO
ADOBE
An adobe of
the Mexican period

The official Steinbeck plaque.

The Lara-Soto Adobe is located on 460 Pierce Street. Francisco Soberanes built the home and later sold it to Jesus Soto. Ownership transferred hands several times until the property was abandoned. It became the hangout for outlaws and became known as the Bandit House. Josephine Blanch remodeled it in the 1940s.

One famous resident was John Steinbeck who lived here in 1944 and sold it one year later. Since then the adobe has been a private residence, a doctor's office and now the Admissions Office for the Monterey Institute of International Studies.

Behind the adobe is a small inviting garden.

Looking North on Pierce Street. There is said to be a grave beneath the massive cypress that dominates the front lawn of the home.

Larkin House

And, pray, who is the tinman?

The chap that owns these stables, and that large block there, and the store in front. I thought everybody knew him. He came here a few years ago—a poor ragged younker, and took to making tin cups and saucepans to earn a living. Well, you see he lived very close for three or four years, grudging himself the smallest comfort, until he scraped together money to buy a large stock of liquor and other things, with which he set up a grog and general store. Since then he's been dabbling in every sort of speculation, not forgetting his original calling (for he manufacturers tin pans for the use of the miners), and they say he's now one of the richest men in Monterey. There isn't one of these saucepans that he turns out of his shop that doesn't fetch at least four dollars; though the same article could be bought, in any part of the States, for five shillings. He's a hard nut to crack, an 'I guess shaves as close to the wind, in a bargain, as the sharpest amongst us Yankees

~ William Redmond Ryan, *Personal Adventures of Upper and Lower California*, 1848

The Larkin House is registered California State Historical Landmark #106, a National Historical Landmark and on the Register of Historic Places.

Vintage 1940s postcard. Pub. Bell Magazine Agency. The Larkin House, Monterey. Thomas Larkin was the only US consul to California under Mexican rule.

Tuesday, July 28. Com. Stockton informed me today that I had been appointed Alcade of Monterey and its jurisdiction. I had dreamed in the course of my life, as most people have, of the thousand things I might become, but it never entered my visions that I should succeed to the dignity of a Spainish alcade….my trunks were packed, my books boxed, and in an hour I was on shore, a guest in the house of our consul T.O. Larkin, Esq., whose munificent hospitalities reach every officer of the squadron, and every functionary in the interest of the flag. This is the more appreciated from the fact that there is not a public table or hotel in all California. High and low, rich and poor, are thrown together on the private liberality of the citizens.

~ Walter Colton, alcade, *Three Years in California*, 1850

Thomas Oliver Larkin came to Monterey after his half brother John Cooper. His home is a two-storey design, which became known as the Monterey Colonial style.

When Thomas Larkin was appointed US consul to Alta California in 1844, his home served as consulate. It was also used as offices for Colton when he was first appointed Alcade of Monterey.

The great-great-granddaughter of Thomas Larkin, Alice Larkin Toulmin, presented the home to the State of California in 1957.

The upper floor shows off the famed interior designer Francis Elkins work, hired by Alice Larkin Toulmin.

The Larkin Garden

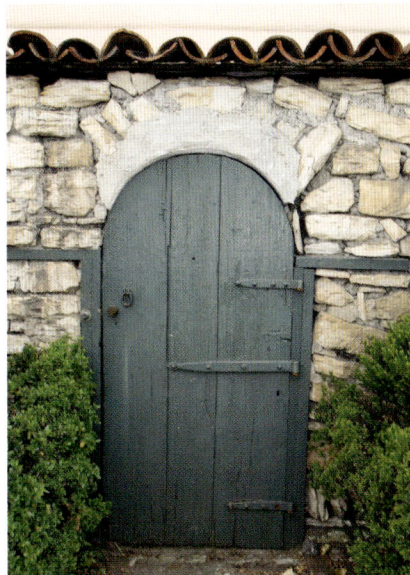

Alice Larkin Toulmin planted the garden in the 1920s through to the 1950s.

The garden was designed to reflect the family's New England Heritage.

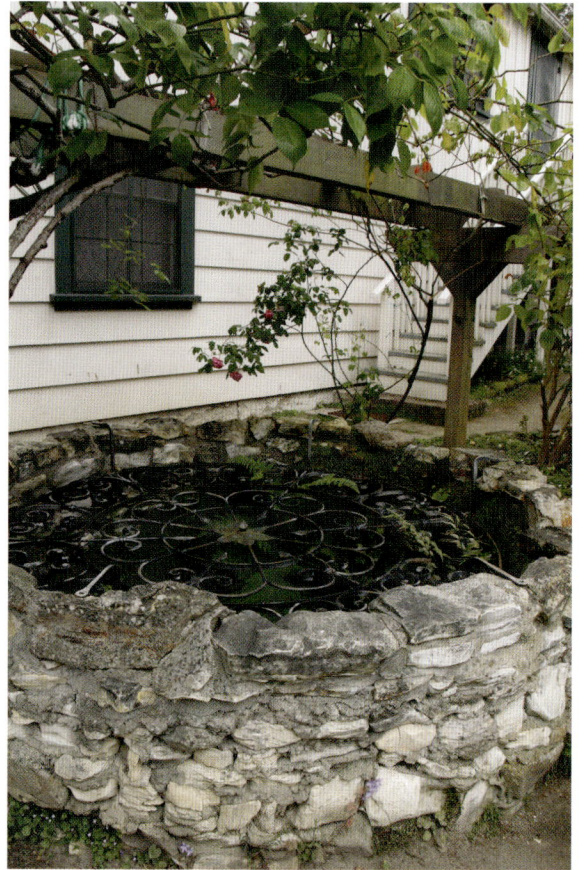

The rose arbor.

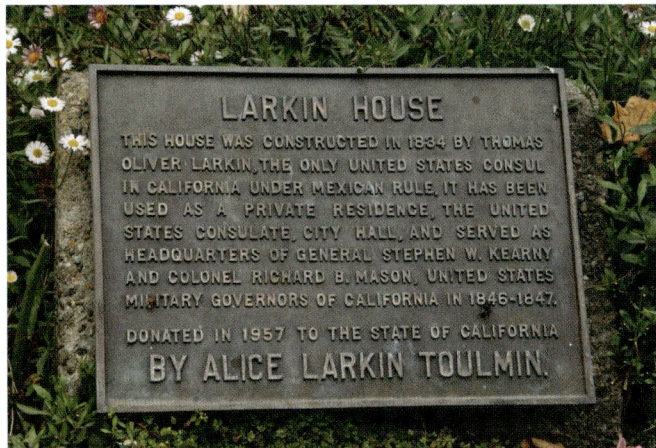

LARKIN HOUSE
THIS HOUSE WAS CONSTRUCTED IN 1834 BY THOMAS
OLIVER LARKIN, THE ONLY UNITED STATES CONSUL
IN CALIFORNIA UNDER MEXICAN RULE. IT HAS BEEN
USED AS A PRIVATE RESIDENCE, THE UNITED
STATES CONSULATE, CITY HALL, AND SERVED AS
HEADQUARTERS OF GENERAL STEPHEN W. KEARNY
AND COLONEL RICHARD B. MASON, UNITED STATES
MILITARY GOVERNORS OF CALIFORNIA IN 1846-1847.

DONATED IN 1957 TO THE STATE OF CALIFORNIA

BY ALICE LARKIN TOULMIN.

The official 1957 plaque.

LARKIN HOUSE

HAS BEEN DESIGNATED A
REGISTERED NATIONAL
HISTORIC LANDMARK

UNDER THE PROVISIONS OF THE
HISTORIC SITES ACT OF AUGUST 21, 1935
THIS SITE POSSESSES EXCEPTIONAL VALUE
IN COMMEMORATING AND ILLUSTRATING
THE HISTORY OF THE UNITED STATES

U. S. DEPARTMENT OF THE INTERIOR
NATIONAL PARK SERVICE

1962

The official 1962 Registered National Historic Landmark plaque.

Madariaga Adobe

The first carnival ball that I attended took place near Monterey in 1829. On this occasion they all had red, black, and green paint ...and cascarones (egg-shells filled with finely cut gold and silver paper), and vials of different colored liquids...It was the great sport to ride against each other, each endeavoring to stain his opponents face while himself escaping. As we neared Monterey the carnival spirit grew wilder, and the ladies dresses and faces suffered, but we all took it in good part.

~ Brigida Briones, "Gold Hunters of California, A Carnival Ball at Monterey in 1829," *The Century Quarterly*, Vol. 41, Issue 3, 1891

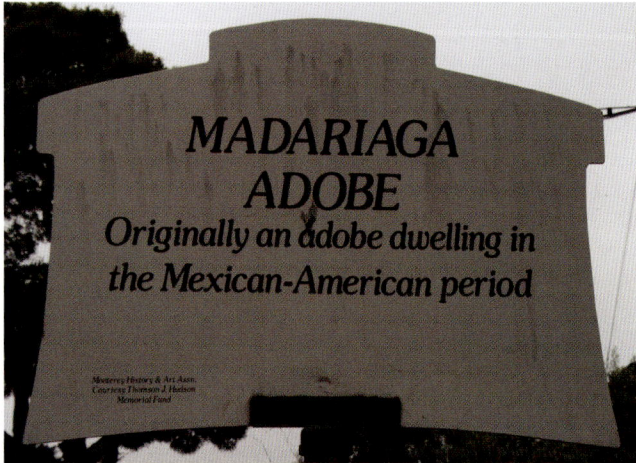

MADARIAGA ADOBE
Originally an adobe dwelling in the Mexican-American period

Monterey History & Art Assn.
Courtesy Thomas J. Hudson
Memorial Fund

The Madariaga Adobe is located at 615 Abrego St. across from Casa Pacheco. Jose Maria Madariaga built the adobe in 1847. Members of the Madariaga family lived there until 1856.

EXIT ONLY
ENTER FROM WEBSTER ST.

Maria Barreto Madariaga was a wealthy widow who inherited her husband's ranch, Rancho el Pescardo, part of present day Pebble Beach. After his death, she sold the 4,000-acre ranch in 1846 for $500. Her second husband Jose Madariaga built her this one story adobe in Monterey.

Mayo Hayes O'Donnell Library

The California landed us at Monterey on the morning of the twenty-third of February, 1849. As the anchor, I think, the first man from shore to spring up the ship's side was ex-United States Consul Thomas O. Larkin. Quickly following him came Captain H.W. Halleck ad, I think, Captain W.T. Sherman of the army. The cut of their clothes would have reminded a tailor of the eastern fashions of a year or two before, but in all other respects they seemed like men on Broadway. This was to be my stopping place for the time being, while most of the passengers went to San Francisco. The hospitality of Mr .Larkin, and afterward of Mr. James Watson, gave me a home at first. It was on Friday that we landed. On Sunday, the twenty-fifth of February, I preached my first sermon in California. It was eleven o'clock in the forenoon, in Colton Hall.

~ S.H. Willey, Presbyterian Minister, Thirty Years in California; a contribution to history of the state from 1849 to 1879

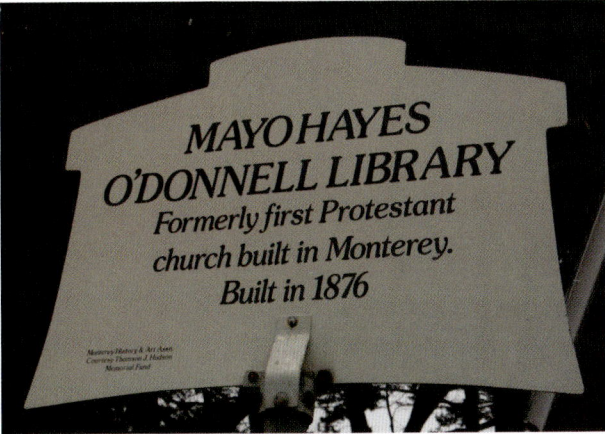

The library was originally the Saint James Episcopal Church.

The church was moved to 155 Van Buren Street to its present location at Pacific Street near Merritt house.

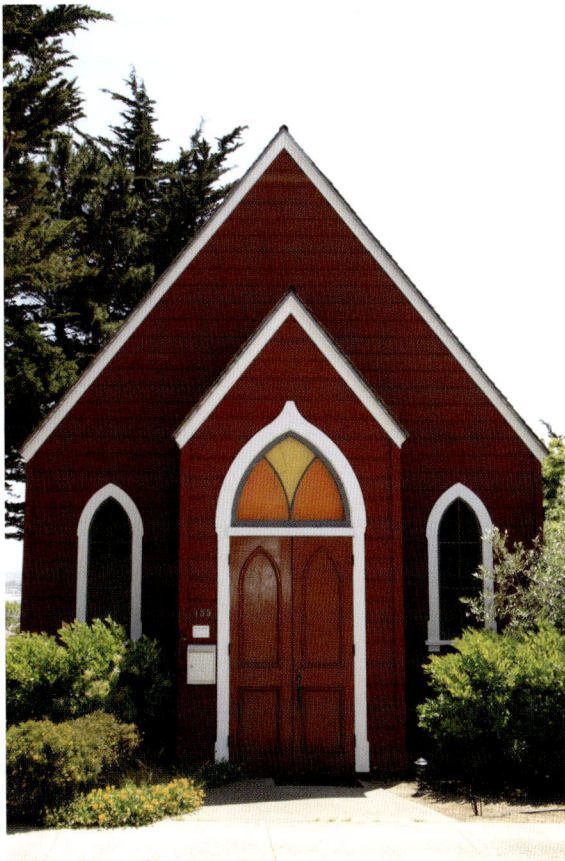

The architectural style of the church is Gothic. It was the first protestant church in Monterey.

The library contains over 2000 books, photographs and documents about the history of Monterey and California.

Merrit House

Some of your politicians talk of giving up California. Why, you can no more give her up, than you can the soil on which you tread. You may say she shall go back to Mexico, but she won't go there; she will be a territory, and then a State, of the American Confederacy, and nothing else. We don't care a fig, how you figure it out on your political map; we have figured it out for ourselves, and our work will stand, what ever may become of yours. Monterey has still Mr. Colton, of the Navy Alcade. He tried hard to get off when his year was up, but the people remonstrated, and addressed communications to Commodore Shubrick and Gov. Mason, and so he consented to remain for the present. The citizens have offered to send for his family, but he has decided to return in the Congress when she goes. His popularity lies in his energy, impartial administration of justice, and the extensive improvements he is effecting in the city. Among these is a large stone edifice, designed for public school. It is a superb building; the citizens call it Colton Hall.

~ William Robert Garner, editor Donald Munro Craig, *Letters from California 1846-1847*, Edited with a sketch of the life and times of their author

The Merrit home is located at 386 Pacific Street.

Merrit house was built in the 1860s by Don Ignacio Vallejo. He later sold the home to Judge Josia Merritt who was the first American Judge of Monterey County. The house was also used as a boarding house.

The formal garden is enhanced with rose bushes lining the brick pathway.

The upper balcony.

Monterey Museum of Art

The Monterey Museum of Art is located at 559 Pacific St., across from Colton Hall.

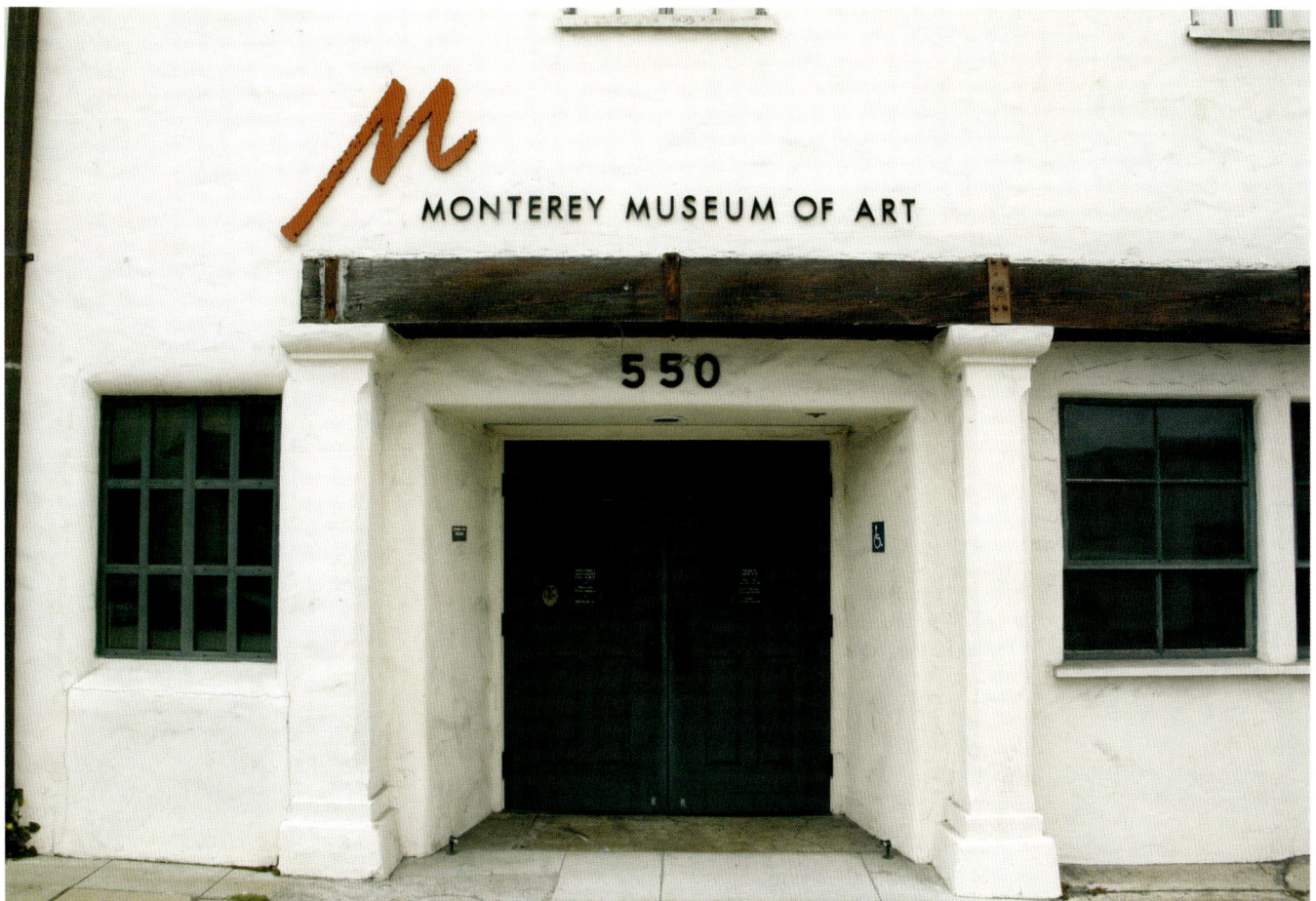

There is a large collection of works by artists who have lived on the peninsula.

Old Monterey Hotel

I could scarcely leave my hotel and turn a corner without being lost, in the tortuous meanderings of the deviating ways of its thoroughfares. A young goose strayed from the flock within the sound of their answering voices screamed and called for half a day, evidently in great trouble, running back and forth and returning every minute to the spot from whence she started. At last I concluded that it was hardly just to expect a goose to know more of these streets than the people do, although hatched and bred within its crooked and uncertain precincts, so I started off and spent half an hour in getting her back to her sympathizing kindred.
~ Caroline M. Churchill, *Over The Purple Hills or Sketches of travel in California, embracing all the important points usually visited by tourists*

The hotel was designed by architect William Weeks.

The old Monterey hotel is located at 406 Alvarado Street.

It was constructed in 1904.

Window detail.

Old Monterey Jail

Native prisoners, arrested for robbery and confined in the adobe jail at Monterey, clamored for their guitars, and the nights were filled with music until the rascals swung at half-mast.
~ 1902 Charles Warren Stoddard, In The Footprints of The Padres

The Old Monterey Jail was built in 1854 and used up until 1956.

Today the cells are set up with props and notes on some of the prisoners kept behind these granite walls.

A detail of the building looking onto Pacific Street.

Osio-Rodriguez Adobe

As the signing went on, gun followed gun from the fort, the echoes reverberating grandly around the bay, till finally, as the loud ring of the thirty-first was heard, there was a shout: 'That's for California!' and everyone joined in giving three times three for the new star added to our Confederation.

~ Bayard Taylor, reporter *New York Tribune, Eldorado or Adventures in the path of Empire,* 1849

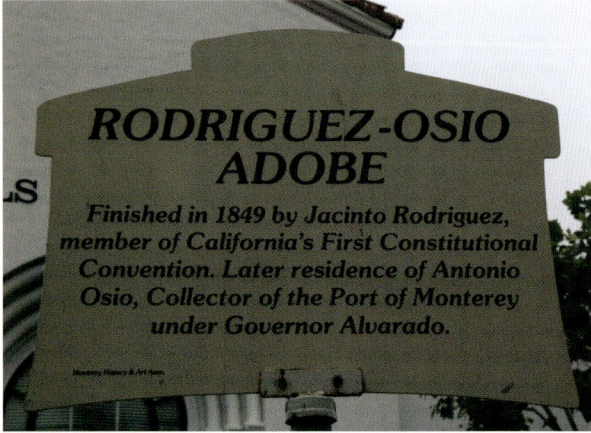

The Osio-Rodriguez adobe is located at 380 Alvarado Street. The adobe is one of the last ones standing on this busy main street.

It was built by Jacinto Rodriguez who was a delegate to the California Constitutional Convention at Colton Hall. Over the years it has seen many uses and currently it is a restaurant

The two story adobe has a grey shake roof, upper balcony with French doors leading out and long narrow windows on the first story.

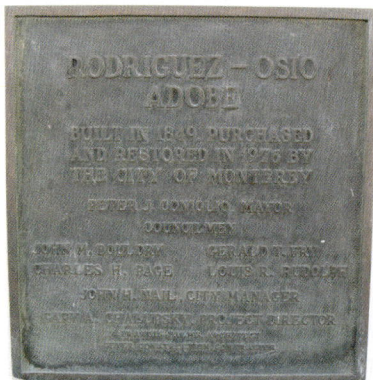

The 1976 official plaque.

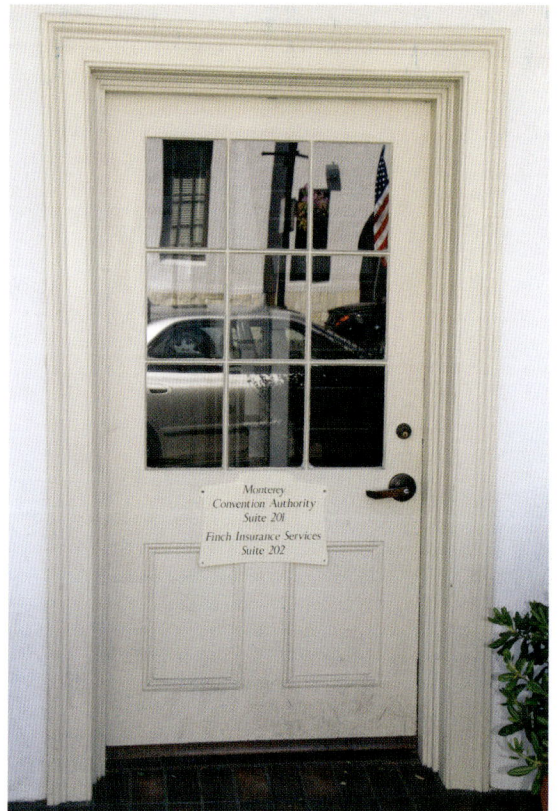

A detail of the door.

Pacific House Museum

The next day we were "turned-to" early, and began taking off the hatches, overhauling the cargo, and getting everything ready for inspection. At eight, the officers of the customs, five in number, come on board, and began examining the cargo, manifest, &c. The Mexican revenue laws are very strict, and require the whole cargo to be landed, examined, and taken on board again: but our agent had succeeded in compounding for the last two vessels, and saving the trouble of taking the cargo ashore.

~ Richard Henry Dana, sailor, *Two Years Before The Mast; a personal narrative*, 1841

The plaza in front of Pacific house. Pacific House is located at 200-222 Calle Principal.

The Pacific House is registered California State Historical Landmark #354. Pacific House was built by David Wright, from the British Isles in 1847 for Thomas Larkin. The U.S. Quartermaster Department used the building for storing supplies. James McKinley bought the house in 1849 and used it as a boarding house and as a store. It was later used as a saloon, dance hall and a county courthouse.

David Jacks purchased Pacific House in 1880 and kept it as a residence. Margaret Jacks gave the house to the State of California in 1954.

The Pacific House with the gate leading into Memory Garden. Directly in front is the Maritime Museum.

A detail of one of the side doors set deep into the adobes thick walls.

Pacific House Balcony

The colorful cutouts, including seafarers bring the Monterey of the 1800s to life.

The archway into Memory Garden. Frederick Law Olmstead Jr. designed the garden. His father is the famed landscape architect who designed Central Park.

A detail of a light fixture.

Memory Garden

Memory Garden was designed in 1927, transforming the old corral into a Spanish style garden. It had been used as a storage place and a site for bear and bull fights.

The central Mediterranean fountain with koi fish and lily pads.

A small garden statue

Spanish arches break the garden into two distinct areas.

Detail of an arch looking into the expanse of the garden. At different seasons of the year camellias, wisteria, climbing roses and even lemons are in bloom.

The seven-foot high wall encloses the courtyard.

The central fountain is framed by four magnolia trees.

Tiled fountain near the barbeque area where receptions and other gatherings are held.

Spring blooms.

The doorway leads to the Sensory Garden, Duarte Store, and Cole House.

Perry- Downer House

The officers were dressed in the costume which we found prevail through the country,--broad brimmed hat, usually of a black or dark brown color, with a gilt or figured band round the crown, and lined under the rim with silk; a short jacket of silk, of figured calico...;the shirt open in the neck; rich waistcoat, if any; pantaloons open at the sides below the knee, laced with gilt, usually of velveteen or broadcloth; or else short breeches and white stockings. They wear the deer-skin shoe, which is of dark brown color, and (being made by Indians) usually a good deal ornamented.

~ 1841 Richard Henry Dana, sailor, Two Years Before The Mast: a personal narrative

PERRY HOUSE

Victorian home build in 1860 by whaling captain Manuel Perry and his wife Mary de Mello Silva, of Boston. The house remained in the family until 1963. Restored in 1967.

Monterey History & Art Assn.

The Perry-Downer House is located at 201 Van Buren Street.

The home is a great example of an early framed house. Captain Manuel Perry built the home in 1860. Originally it was a single story dwelling but a second story was added at the turn of the century.

Today the Perry-Downer home contains a 5,000+ costume collection devoted entirely to apparel relating to the history of the Monterey Peninsula and the State of California.

The home was restored by Maggie and Webster Downer in 1967.

The garden behind the home. The carriage house was originally a garden shed. The stain glass ceiling was bought in San Francisco

The home today is a beautiful example of Victorian architecture with large windows and this special octagonal one on the front.

Both front doors are embellished with a P for Perry monogram.

Portola Memorial

Detail of dedication plaque.

The official commemorative plaque for Don Gaspar de Portola who
founded the Presidio and Settlement of Monterey on June 3 1770. He
served in Monterey as Mexico's first governor of Alta California.

The gateway to the Presidio.

Royal Presido Chapel

May 11, we drove to Monterey, where the United States flag was first raised on the Pacific Coast. A deep sleep fell upon the town soon after its birth. The adobe houses are nodding into the streets through which the wash of the bay resounds like a snore. The backbone of a whale, long dead, forms the walk up a weedy way to the old church, and with in the mouldering structure all is as dead as the whale, save a window of rich stained glass which lightens up the chancel with the hope of a better life.

~ Thomas S. Chard, traveler, *California Sketches*, Chicago, 1888. He traveled from Chicago to California in 1888

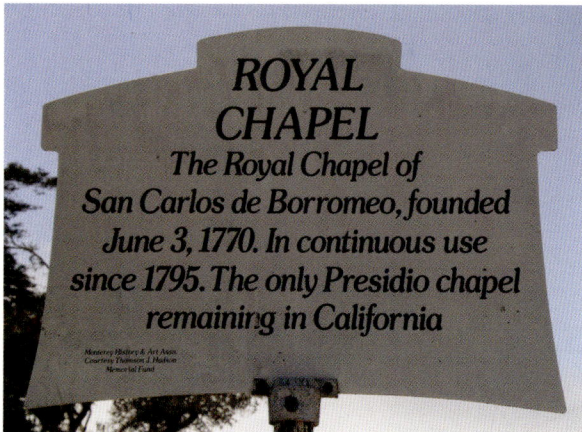

ROYAL CHAPEL
The Royal Chapel of San Carlos de Borromeo, founded June 3, 1770. In continuous use since 1795. The only Presidio chapel remaining in California

Monterey History & Art Assn. Courtesy Thomson J. Hudson Memorial Fund

The Royal Presidio Chapel of San Carlos Borromeo Monterey is registered California State Historical Landmark #105, a National Historical Landmark and on the Register of Historic Places.

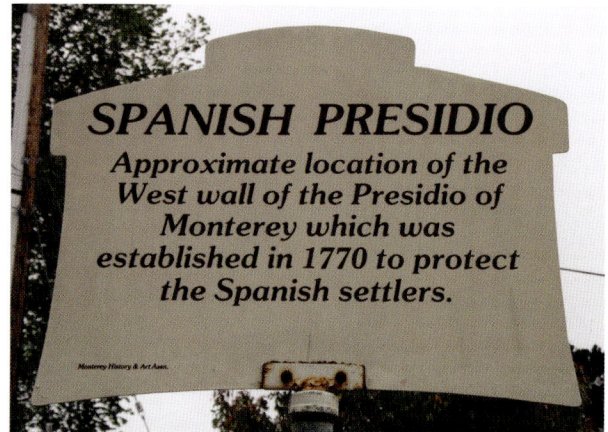

SPANISH PRESIDIO
Approximate location of the West wall of the Presidio of Monterey which was established in 1770 to protect the Spanish settlers.

Monterey History & Art Assn.

By 1817, almost 50 years after Monterey was founded, settlers began building their homes outside the safety of the presidio walls. Today only the Royal Presidio Chapel remains at this site.

The chapel, completed in 1795, is the oldest continuously operating church in California. The chapel was build by local Indians. Manuel Ruiz, a native of Guadalajara Mexico, supervised the work.

Looking heavenwards. The statue of Our Lady of Guadalupe used to stand in the niche at the top of the church, but was removed for conservation. The statue had been in place since 1794.

The chapel was founded while California was still a Spanish colony. Later, Father Junipero Serra would move the church from Monterey to Carmel. The close proximity of the chapel to the Presidio was a major motivating factor for this decision.

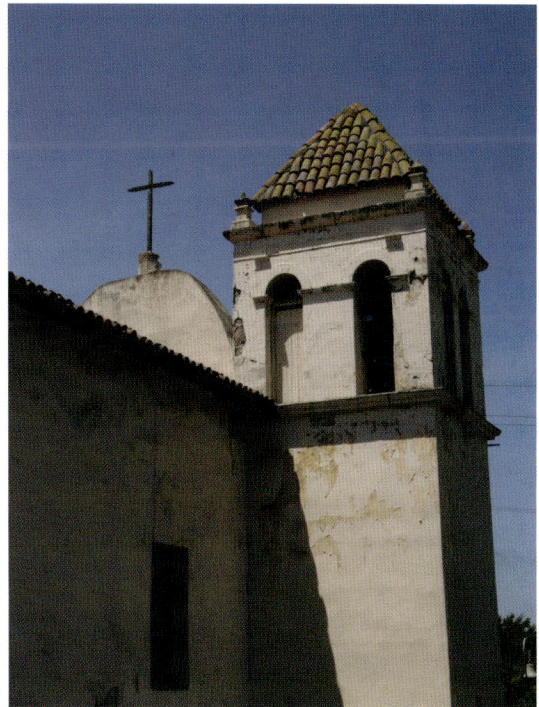

The chapel is also known as the San Carlos Cathedral. John Steinbeck refers to the chapel in *Tortilla Flats*.

The bells.

Detail of the west side door. According to the docents at the site, the surroundings may have originally come from the Carmel mission.

The Father Serra statue is located behind the chapel in the garden by Fremont Street.

Around the chapel look for the statues of St. John, the Sorrowful Mother and the Spanish Madonna.

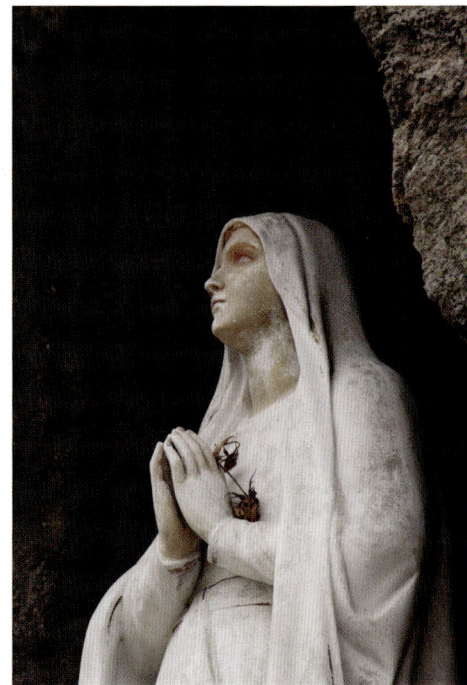

The Lourdes grotto was constructed in 1921.

Robert Louis Stevenson House

The Monterey of last year exists no longer. A huge hotel has sprung up in the desert by the railway. Three sets of diners sit down successively to table. Invaluable toilettes figure along the beach and between the live oaks; and Monterey is advertised in the newspapers, and posted in the waiting rooms at railway stations, as a resort for wealth and fashion. Alas for the little town!
~ R.L. Stevenson, *Across The Plains*, 1880, Chattus & Windus, London, 1892

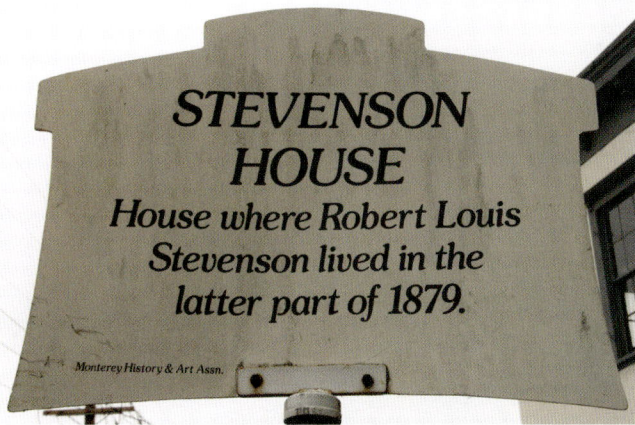

The Robert Louis Stevenson House is located at 530 Houston Street. Dona Rafael Gonzales who used the building as a warehouse originally owned the home. Robert Louis Stevenson stayed here for a mere 3 months, though some sources put it at 4 months. It was then known as the French Hotel.

Robert Louis Stevenson House, Monterey. Pub. Bell Magazine Agency.

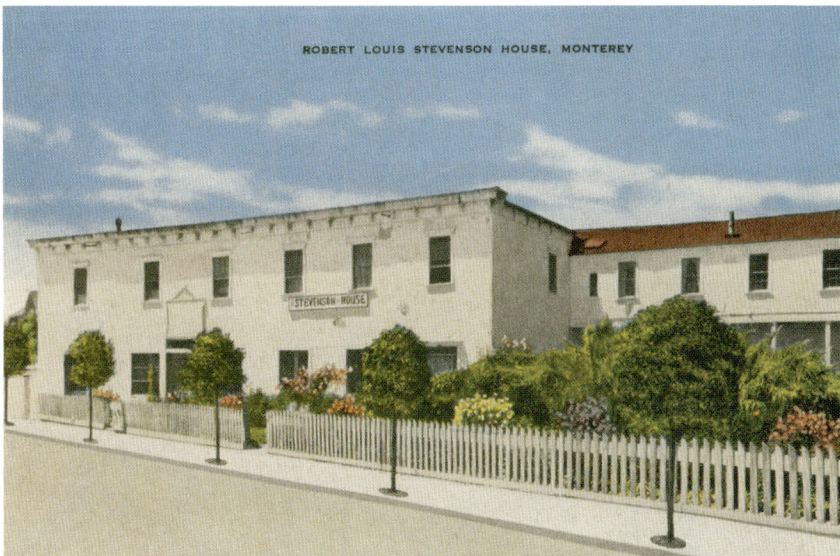

The Robert Louis Stevenson House is registered California State Historical Landmark #352 and on the Register of Historic Places. The property became state owned in 1941.

A view from the street. Robert L. Stevenson lived in the home for a mere 3 months when he was courting his future wife, Fanny Osbourne. The home has a large collection of his belongings including a folding table, which was a wedding gift to the couple from his parents.

A side view showing the garden entrance.

Detail of door with the French Hotel sign above. When R.L Stevenson lived here, waiting for his future wife Fanny's divorce to be finalized, it was a rooming house.

Robert Louis Stevenson Garden

Behind the home one of the winding paths invites the visitor to explore this exquisite garden.

The Flowers
All the names I know from nurse:
Gardener's garters, Shepherd's purse;
Bachelor's buttons, Lady's smock,
And the Lady Hollyhock.
Fairy places, fairy things,
Fairy woods where the wild bee wings,
Tiny trees for tiny dames-
These must be all fairy names!
Tiny woods below whose boughs
Shady fairies weave a house;
Tiny tree-tops, rose or thyme,
Where the braver fairies climb!
Fair are grown-up people's trees,
But the fairest woods are these;
Where if I were not so tall,
I should live for good and all.

~ Robert Louis Stevenson

The official dedication plaque.

The Robert Louis Stevenson garden is a romantic English garden with winding paths and free forming beds.

It doesn't matter in which direction you look, for blooms are abundant.

While in the garden it doesn't seem possible that a gasoline station and bus stop are literally just outside the back gate.

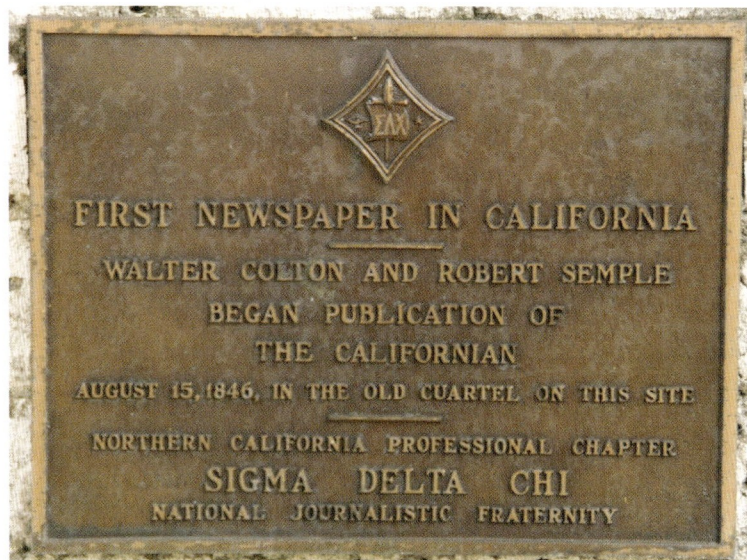

Dedication plaque for the first newspaper in California, which was written in both Spanish and English, and each issue sold for one bit, or 12.5 cents.

Our paper, the only one published in California, made its hebdomadal appearance again to-day. It is a little fellow, but is half filled or more with original matter. A paper is much like an infant; the smaller it is, the more anxious the attentions which it requires.
~Walter Colton, alcade. *Three Years in California*, 1850

Back gate.

Sloat's Landing

I declare to the inhabitants of California, that although I come in arms with a powerful force, I do not come among them as an enemy to California; on the contrary, I come as their best friend – as henceforward California will be a portion of the United States...
~ Commodore John D. Sloat at the harbor of Monterey, July 7, 1846, Steven R. Butler, editor, *A Documentary History of the Mexican War*, 1995, p.146

Sloat's Landing

On this spot on July 7, 1846, U.S. Marines and Sailors landed and raised the American flag over the Custom House which stands before you. Mexico and the United States were at war. American forces landing in Monterey claimed 600,000 square miles of land for the United States.

This plaque commemorates the place where Commodore John Drake Sloat raised the first American flag in the area.

Stokes Adobe

The land, mile after mile around Monterey is owned by the Southern Pacific, a mammoth corporation controlling many railroads and street-car lines as well as lands and hotel in California, although often in their names. The Drive is kept in order by the sub-heading of the same corporation, "The Pacific Improvement Company," the apple of whose eye is the Hotel Del Monte; a Paradisical Symphony in architecture and gardening.
~ T. S. Kenderine, traveler, *California Revisited 1858-1897*, 1897

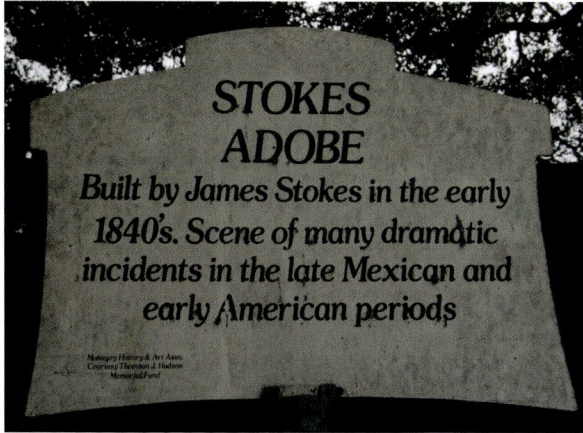

The Stokes adobe is located at 500 Hartnell. Dr. James Stokes built this home c.1840. He was a former mayor of Monterey, a physician, and he ran a general store.

The home was expanded from a one-room adobe into a two-story adobe for his wife and children. The Stokes home was the site of many important events such as the annual Monterey Cascarone ball. The home was later sold to Honore Escolle in 1856, who is credited with opening Monterey's first bakery.

Detail of door.

The building has been used as a home, a garrison for officers and as a restaurant. Perhaps while enjoying your meal you might hear the ghostly cries of a child as the building is said to be haunted.

The stone wall around the compound.

Thomas Cole House

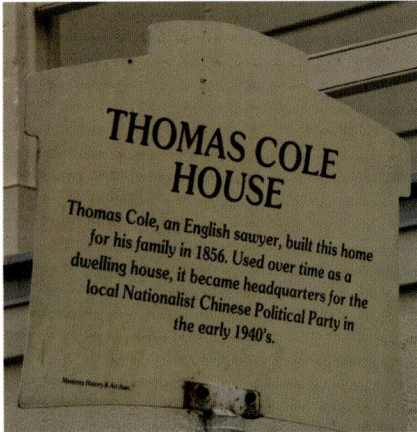

The Thomas Cole house is located on Olivier Street and Custom House Plaza. It is right next door to Duarte's Store.

The home was constructed by Thomas Cole in 1856. It features a shake roof, an upper balcony and two simple windows on the front. The building is currently being renovated.

The home was used as a boarding house and as headquarters for the local National Chinese Political Party in the early 1940s.

The Thomas Cole House and its neighbor Duarte's Store.

Underwood Brown Adobe

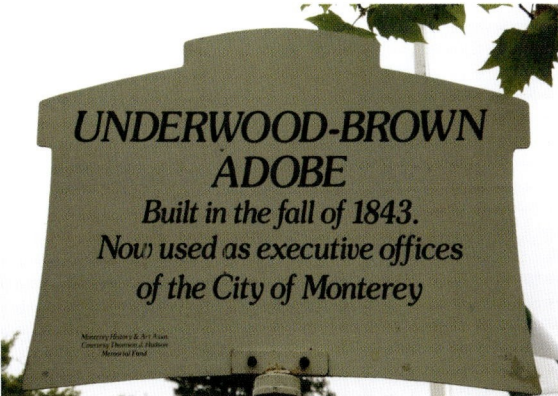

UNDERWOOD-BROWN ADOBE
Built in the fall of 1843.
Now used as executive offices
of the City of Monterey

Monterey History & Art Assn.
Courtesy Thornton J. Hudson
Memorial Fund

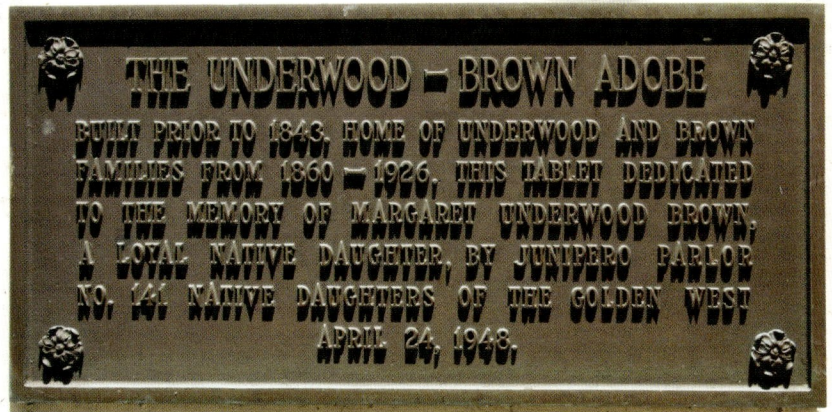

THE UNDERWOOD – BROWN ADOBE
BUILT PRIOR TO 1843. HOME OF UNDERWOOD AND BROWN
FAMILIES FROM 1860 – 1926. THIS TABLET DEDICATED
TO THE MEMORY OF MARGARET UNDERWOOD BROWN,
A LOYAL NATIVE DAUGHTER, BY JUNIPERO PARLOR
NO. 141 NATIVE DAUGHTERS OF THE GOLDEN WEST
APRIL 24, 1948.

The building is located at Pacific and Madison streets. Santiago Stokes, a former Alcade of Monterey, constructed it. The adobe is named for it's longest occupants, Charles Underwood and his daughter Margaret Brown.

The Underwood-Brown was built in 1843. The City of Monterey acquired the adobe in 1934.

Currently the adobe is used for city offices.

The carved doorway is from Mexico and was installed in the 1970s.

Underwood Brown Adobe Gardens

Behind the adobe is a landscaped garden and verandah connecting the home to more city offices.

Tiled map on one of the garden walls showing Alta California.

Vasquez Adobe

A spirit of hatred and revenge took possession of me. I had numerous fights in defense of what I believed to be my rights and those of my countrymen. I believed we were unjustly deprived of the social rights that belonged to us.
~ E. T. Sawyer, *Tiburcio Vasquez, The Life and Career of Tiburicio Vasquez, The California Stage Robber.* The quote was the last statement he made before he was hung.

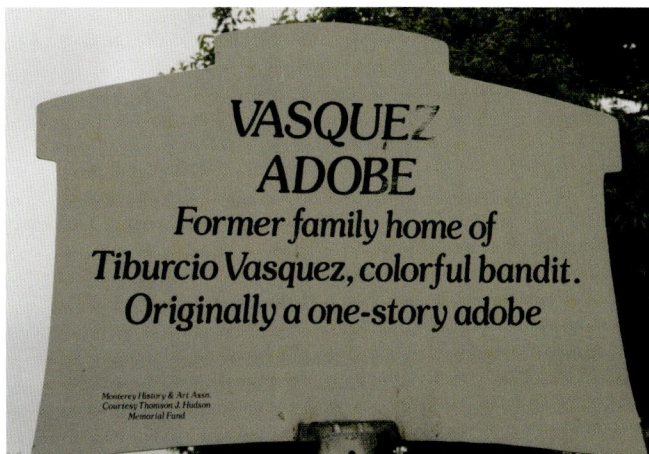

VASQUEZ ADOBE
Former family home of
Tiburcio Vasquez, colorful bandit.
Originally a one-story adobe

Monterey History & Art Assn.
Courtesy Thomson J. Hudson
Memorial Fund

The Vasquez Adobe is registered California State Historical Landmark #351. It is located at 546 Dutra St.

The Vasquez Adobe was home to Tiburcio Vasquez (1837-1875), a desperado born into a well-to-do Monterey family. His exploits included holding up stagecoaches, rustling cattle, and even stabbing a Sheriff. The home was altered significantly in the 1900s by Louis Hill, the son of James Hill, president of the Great Northern Railway, from a one-story adobe into a two-story adobe, with shake roof and upper verandah.

Vizcaino Landing Site

The land is well populated with Indians without number, many of whom came on different occasions to our camp. They seem to be gentle and peaceful people; they say with signs that there are many villages inland. The sustenance which these Indians eat most daily, besides fish and shellfish, is acorns and another fruit larger than a chestnut, this is what we could understand of them.

~ Sebastien Vizcaino, Monterey Bay, 1602

A detail of the monument.

The landing place of Sebastian Vizcaino and Fray Junipero Serra is registered California State Historical Landmark #128, a National Historical Landmark, and on the Register of Historic Places. The monument is dedicated to Father Junipero Serra, who came to Vizcaino's landing spot 168 years later.

The Father Serra monument.

A Short Drive From Town

There are two attractions in the vicinity, without which I fear Monterey would have ultimately passed from the memory of man. These are the mission at Carmelo and the Druid grove at Cypress Point. In the edge of the town there is a cross which marks the spot where Padre Junipero Sera sang his first Mass at Monterey. It was a desolate picture when I last saw it. It stood but a few yards from the sea, in a lonely hollow. It was a favorite subject with the artists who found their way thither, and who were wont to paint it upon the seashells that lay almost within reach. Now a marble statue of Junipero Serra, erected by Mrs. Leland Stanford, marks the spot.
~ Charles Warren Stoddard, *In The Footprints of The Padres*, 1902

17 Mile Drive Snapshots

The one great feature of the place is a drive of seventeen miles, partly by sea, over cliff and rock, and returning through a bosky del. Here the "breaking waves dash high," and it is indeed "on a stern and rock-bound coast." The gentle Pacific belies her name and sets at defiance her traditions, for the great waves rush in mad fury fifty feet high, then break and scatter, reflecting in the sunlight their splendor, making a hundred ere they reach the sandy beach. Down the long line of ages has this wondrous spectacle been each day repeating its magnificence, and to the end.
~ Mary H. Wills, *A Winter in California*, 1889. Mary H. Wills of Pennsylvania spent one year traveling in California.

ALONG 17 MILE DRIVE
MONTEREY PENINSULA,
CALIFORNIA—M12

Space fails to enumerate all the attractions of this sylvan retreat, but among them, and of the proper things to do is to take the Seventeen-mile Drive, a road that includes a succession of beautiful views, both inland and of the ocean, also a visit to Monterey, Pacific Grove and the Carmel Mission. Inspiring scenes all, but on returning to the winding, shady avenue of the Del Monte we experience a fresh delight which is almost a surprise that the place is so surpassing lovely. Can anything else compare with it? Does anything like it exist on this planet? Can even Paradise be fairer?
~ Susie C. Clark, traveler, *The Round Trip from the Hub to the Golden Gate*, 1890

Vintage 1940s postcard. Pub. Bell Magazine Agency.
Pinnacle Point, 17 Mile Drive

Vintage 1940s postcard. Pub. Bell Magazine Agency. Seal and Bird rock, 17 Mile Drive.

Unchanged Vistas

It was 4 P.M. before we reach our destination on the siding at Hotel Del Monte. Here we found carriages in waiting to take us on the seventeen-mile drive around the coast. They had not gone far before the heavy fogs again rolled in from the ocean and made wraps and overcoats very comfortable. …Their route first led through the old town of Monterey, whose old adobe and historic buildings attracted general attention. Al-though a town of only 2000 inhabitants, it looks most prosperous and they were not surprised to learn that it possesses fine schools, electric lights, a good water system, a bank and a public park, besides an up-to-date trolley line, and is also the site of a large military post.

~ Clifford Paynter Allen, traveler, Pilgrimage of Mary commandery no. 36 Knights Templar of Pennsylvania to the Twenty-ninth triennial conclave of the Grand Encampment U.S. at San Francisco, Cal., 1904.

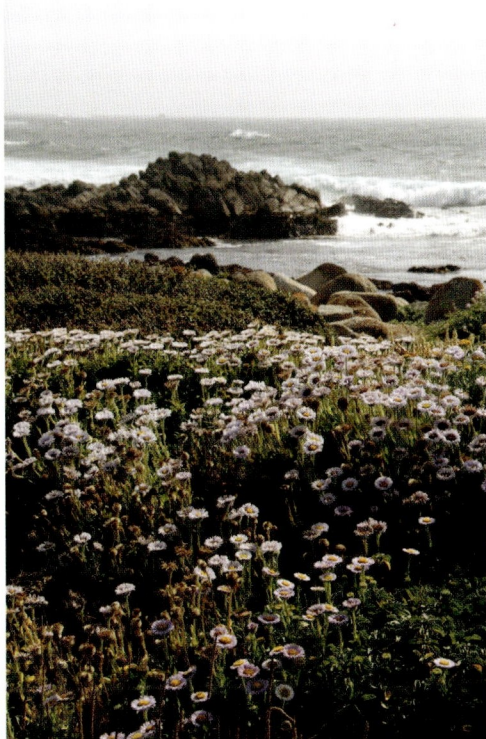

A lush meadow leading to the sea.

The sandy beach with those famous waves.

The water breaks over the rocks and is dashed into foamy spray, high into the air.

Bird Rock, one of the 21 points-of-interest stops along 17-Mile Drive.

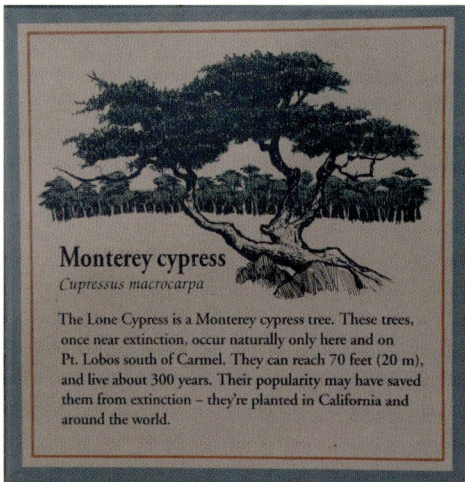

Monterey cypress

Cupressus macrocarpa

The Lone Cypress is a Monterey cypress tree. These trees, once near extinction, occur naturally only here and on Pt. Lobos south of Carmel. They can reach 70 feet (20 m), and live about 300 years. Their popularity may have saved them from extinction – they're planted in California and around the world.

Monterey Cyprus plaque.

Having passed the seal rocks, we came in our drive to groves of cypress trees. The Monterey Cyprus is a curious tree. It starts out well enough from the ground, but when its trunk is a dozen feet in the air, it suddenly remembers that it has a pressing engagement in the direction contrary to that of the prevailing wind. We saw a great many trees, the tops of which appeared to be a dozen feet away from their centers of gravity.

~ Thomas S. Chard, traveler, *California Sketches*, 1888

A stunning view of the Cyprus and the ocean.

Destination Carmel

Carmel Mission Basilica
(San Carlos Borromeo de Carmelo Mission)

The church is roofless and ruinous, sea-breezes and sea-fogs, and the alternation of the rain and sunshine, daily widening the breaches and casting the crockets from the wall. As an antiquity in this new land, a quaint specimen of missionary architecture in this new land.

~ R. L. Stevenson, Across The Plains, 1892

San Carlos Mission, Carmel Pub. Bell Magazine Agency. The Mission San Carlos Borromeo de Carmelo is registered California State Historical Landmark #135, a National Historical Landmark and on the Register of Historic Places. The mission is located at Lausen Drive and Rio Road, Carmel.

Attempts at restoration were made in 1884 and 1924 but met with no success. The mission would have to wait until 1931 when a research and restoration program began.

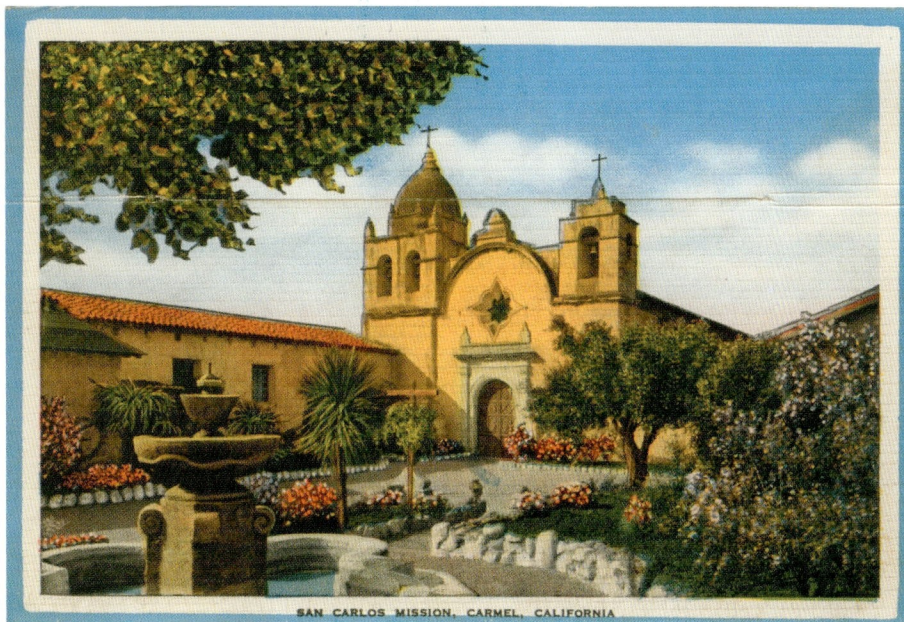

SAN CARLOS MISSION, CARMEL, CALIFORNIA

The Carmel mission was abandoned in 1836 and its lands sold off.

The mission operated for more than 30 years and was an important link in the chain of nine missions that stretched up the Californian coast.

A well-traveled road, leading over the hills, conducted us to the Mission, which is situated on the Pacific side of the promontory, at the head of a shallow bay. The beautiful but deserted valley in which it stands is threaded by the Rio de Carmel, whose waters once gave unfailing fertility to its now neglected gardens. The Mission building is in the form of a hollow square, with a spacious court-yard, overlooked by a heavy belfry and chapel-dome of sun-dried bricks. ...We climbed into the tower and struck the fine old Spanish bells, but the sound called no faces into the blank windows.

~ Bayard Taylor, *Eldorado or Adventures in the Path of Empire*
Writer, 1850

The large quadrangle behind the mission.

The church is named for Saint Charles Borromeo.

There was not a man in the village. They were all away at work, farming or fishing. This little handful of people are living on land to which they have no shadow or title, and from which they may be driven any day,--these Carmel Mission lands having been rented out, by their present owner, in great dairy farms. The parish priest of Monterey told me much of the pitiable condition of these remnants of the San Carlos Indians. He can do little or nothing for them, though their condition makes his heart ache daily: "They have their homes there only by the patience of the thief; it may be that the patience do not last to-morrow."

~ Helen Hunt Jackson, *Glimpses of California and the Missions*, 1883. The phrase is worth preserving; it embodies so much history, history of two races.

In the early 1930s the greatest period of restoration began. Looking at the beautiful mission and the buildings around the quadrant it is hard to imagine that this all once lay in ruin.

> Once in the year, on San Carlos' Day, Mass is sung in the only habitable corner of the ruin; the Indians and the natives gather from all quarters, and light candles among the graves…; then they go their way, and the owl returns and the weeds grow ranker…
> ~ Charles Warren Stoddard, *In The Footprints of The Padres*, 1902

Beautifully maintained gardens ring the mission and outer buildings.

There are many sculptures throughout the gardens.

Sources

Books

Hague, Harlan and Langum, David. *Thomas O. Larkin A life of Patriotism and Profit in Old California*. Norman: University of Oklahoma Press 1990.

Hicks, John, and Hicks, Regina. *Cannery Row- A Pictorial History*. Creative Books, 1972.

Johnston, Robert B. *Old Monterey County- A Pictorial History*. Monterey: Monterey Savings and Loan Association, 1970.

Monterey's Adobe Heritage. Monterey: Monterey Savings and Loan Association, 1965.

Powers, Laura Bride. *Old Monterey; California's Adobe Capital*. San Carlos Press, San Francisco. 1934.

Tays, George, *1900-1958. The Larkin House*. Berkeley: Works Progress administration, 1936.

The Larkin Papers 1822-1858, University of California Press, 1955.

Watkins, Major Rolin G. *History of Monterey & Santa Cruz Counties. California*. Chicago: S.J Clarke Publishing Co., 1925.

Newspapers

Monterey Cypress
Monterey Peninsula Herald

Internet Site

"Spotlight on California's First Theatre & The Troupers of The Gold Coats." http://www.mctaweb.org/spotlight/00/Mar00_CalFirst/cal.html

Resources

Monterey Peninsula
www.mpcc.com

Monterey's Visitors Center
831-649-1770

Monterey County Convention & Visitors Bureau
150 Olivier St 831-657-6400

Monterey History & Art Association
www.montereyhistory.org

Historic Monterey
www.historicmonterey.org

Historic Garden League
www.historicgardenleague.org